Advance Praise for *Spotting Danger Before It Spots Your Teens*

Once again, Gary Quesenberry has hit the nail on the head with his most recent book in his Spotting Danger series. Never before have teens been so vulnerable to violence as they are today. Gary, who has raised three children to adulthood, knows all too well the difficulty and dangers that teens face online, in school, in their cars, in malls, and on the street. Gary crams this book with ten chapters that address such issues as the teen's mind, situational awareness, the power of intuition, visualization, driver safety, and much, much more. Gary's previous books prove he knows his stuff. As a long-time student of violence and predatory mindset and with a long career as a federal air marshal, the man brings a wealth of experience to his writing. Get this one.

—Loren W. Christensen, author, retired police officer,
Vietnam veteran, 10th dan American Freestyle Karate,
and inductee into the Martial Arts Masters Hall of Fame

Every parent of a teen needs to read this book! Gary has so artfully presented the material in a way that is relevant to today's teens and their parents. This is the kind of book you can read with your kids or have them read . . . and they'll even enjoy reading it too (even if they roll their eyes [at first]!).

Gary includes information on how your teen's brain works in this stage of development and how it might make them more vulnerable, which is a crucial part of understanding how to keep them safe. This book is a mix of proven research, Gary's lifelong experience as a former federal air marshal, and lessons he's learned as a dad of three.

Today's world is more complicated and confusing than it's ever been, and *Spotting Danger Before It Spots Your Teens* is a vital tool for every parent of a teen to have in their toolbox. As a parent of two teens, it's in mine.

—Robbin McManne parenting expert, author, founder of Parenting
for Connection, podcast host of *Parenting Our Future*

This is the third in a series of situational awareness books by Gary Quesenberry (retired federal air marshal) and is my favorite one. I wish I'd had this available to me in the past.

I like to make notes and highlight interesting and useful parts in a book, so if you're like me, this book will not disappoint. Gary shares what he has learned from his professional and family life, and this book really does have it all, a blueprint for parents and teens.

Each chapter is well written, is easy to read, provides real-life examples and practical exercises, and finishes with the key points (which I love). This book has helped me, my family, my clients, and my clients' families and can help you become a better protector and parent.

—Nigel Wright, security and family management
consultant—French Riviera

This book is unlike anything on the market regarding safety for not just families but specifically for that critical time when your child is transitioning into a young adult. So much is happening, and as parents it can be hard to have conversations that impact them. Gary does an amazing job of providing a detailed roadmap to help parents ensure they are passing on knowledge that will impart lifesaving skills to their teenagers.

Gary's book breaks down fundamental [situational awareness] skills to surviving and overcoming threats both in person and online. It provides parents with conversation starters for their family and covers how to explain the concepts in an engaging way through scenario-based training for teens.

Spotting Danger Before It Spots Your Teens is a must-read for any parent or for those who are involved with kids who want to help them develop their situational awareness skills.

As both a family safety expert and a parent to young children, I highly recommend this as a must-read for anybody involved with teenagers. We are all vulnerable at times, but being able to recognize those vulnerabilities and being confident in your ability to spot the danger and have a plan is vital.

—Ashley Glinka, former Federal Air Marshal, family safety expert, founder and creator of Child and Parent Empowerment Program (C.A.P.E), co-founder and trainer at CT3.US

Gary is doing some of the most important fundamental work for living a life of ease for both parents and kids. He's a total pro, a loving father, and an authority who communicates from a place of experience and deep caring. His words are not theoretical. This work is about more than just spotting danger; it's about learning to steer in the direction of opportunity and growth. These skills are fundamental for all ages, especially for the teen years when kids are testing their freedom and learning about the world and themselves. Give yourself some relief, knowing that your loved ones are able to make good decisions and that they can be out in the world safely and responsibly.

—Matt Lucas, martial artist, stunt performer, owner of Yama Systems LLC, trainer and bodyworker for AMC's *Into the Badlands* and *Matrix 4*, lead stunt performer for *Into the Badlands Season 3*

Situational awareness is the most important mental self-defense skill in the world, and one of the most difficult to teach. Mr. Quesenberry manages it by distilling decades of real-world experience into a set of knowledge and techniques the layperson can understand. In this third book of his series, he approaches with laser-like focus the challenges of raising safe teens. Every parent of a teen needs this book today. Every parent of a younger child should read it now so they have more time to get ready.

One of the things I particularly appreciate about Mr. Quesenberry's work is his understanding of the civilian mindset. The majority of books by safety professionals, soldiers, and law enforcement approach the lesson from the mindset of a violence professional. They assume a level of knowledge, interest, and capacity for violence that is (thankfully) missing from civilian parents. Mr. Quesenberry's Heads Up series avoids that mistake. He meets parents where they are and provides instruction and advice for the world they live in.

—Jason Brick, 6th degree black belt, host of *Safest Family on the Block*,
author of the *Safest Family on the Block* newsletter,
and bestselling author of *Safe Home Blueprint*

Gary has done it again and delivered a book that should be required reading for parents. Navigating the teenage years is tough for both the parents and the teenager. It's when young adults need to start working on their own life skills in order to have a successful launch in to full adulthood. Personal safety should be at the top of their skill building priority list. This book is the bridge between children and their parent's desire to teach important safety skills, a desire that is sometimes be dismissed by their own children as overcautious.

—Kelly Sayre, author, founder and president of The Diamond Arrow
Group, author of *Sharp Women: Embrace Your Intuition, Build
Your Situational Awareness, & Live Life Unafraid*

Spotting Danger Before It Spots Your Teens should be a must-read for every teenager and every parent of teenagers. The stories of teenagers who found themselves in a dangerous situation but because of their situational awareness skills made it through safely are an immediate help and encouragement. Add to that the steps you can take right now, which are listed throughout the book, and just a few chapters in, you are acquiring and learning skills that keep you and your teenager safer.

Having read Gary's first two books on situational awareness and having Gary as a part of our congregation has made our church a harder target and safer place. Gary sharing with our security team opened our eyes to some immediate changes that had to be made in the way we view church security.

I promise you Gary's knowledge of situational awareness will keep you, your small children, your teenagers, and your organization safer. But don't take my word for it, read the book!

—Wendell Horton, senior pastor, Skyview Missionary
Baptist Church, Fancy Gap, Virginia

As a father of six, *Spotting Danger Before It Spots Your Teens* has significantly impacted my family in a profoundly positive way. In this especially timely book, author Gary Quesenberry delivers relevant, effective, and easy-to-use information to equip both parents *and* teenagers for success in this often volatile, rapidly evolving, dangerous world. As parents, we are not issued "owner's manuals" at the time our children are born. For so many parents, the teenage years pose an especially challenging period when it comes to effective communication and fruitful dialogue. This book is an exceptional resource and guide to successfully addressing the most important topic for a parent, keeping our children safe—to include when we are *not* present. Gary is exceptionally qualified to speak on security-related topics given his extensive experience as a Federal Air Marshal and conducting low-profile missions globally. Success on those missions relied heavily on his behavioral detection skills to spot danger and pre-incident indicators *before* violence happened. Similarly, and as the title implies, *Spotting Danger Before It Spots Your Teens* covers what to do before threats targeting your children fully develop. Keeping our kids safe is non-negotiable. Gary has written a classic book that will impact society and families in an immeasurably significant way.

> —Maury Abreu, CEO/chief instructor at Omega Protective Concepts, former sergeant in the United States Marine Corps, former Federal Corrections Officer (Federal Bureau of Prisons), and former Supervisory Federal Air Marshal (Department of Homeland Security)

Quesenberry's newest book, *Spotting Danger Before It Spots Your Teens,* is a comprehensive approach to safety and situational awareness crafted for the protection of your kids. The time-tested lessons presented here have been proven from middle America to the Middle East at mitigating risk and getting people home safely. This book transcends threat environments and can be guaranteed to help anyone who is willing to apply the lessons within. Gary's real-world experience in counterterrorism and as a loving father, coupled with his contagious passion for training others, shines through in this book. All parents want what's best for their child's safety and security, but many don't know where to get the right answers appropriately scaled for their family—until now.

> —Peter M. Johnson, former Federal Air Marshal, veteran, small business owner, National Law Enforcement Trainer

Gary does a phenomenal job in *Spotting Danger Before It Spots Your Teens* by taking readers through a journey of knowledge, understanding, and practice. He combines real-life stories and personal knowledge with research to support his approach. The book is full of relatable stories relatable that help the reader understand Gary's perspectives and techniques. Lastly, readers learn to develop and apply an awareness plan that can prevent a tragedy and even save lives. Without a doubt, this is a book every parent should buy even if their children have not yet reached their teens.

> —Gabby Franco, Olympian, firearms instructor, competitive shooter

As a twenty-five-year law enforcement veteran and parent of three, situational awareness has been massively important to me both personally and professionally. The same skills I've developed as a law enforcement professional are equally as important in keeping my family safe when I'm off duty. Unfortunately, as a parent there comes a time when our teenagers venture out into this sometimes-dangerous world no longer under our watchful eye. One of the most valuable lessons we can instill in our children is to be aware of their surroundings and teach them practical tools to deal with potential threats.

What I love about Gary's most recent book, *Spotting Danger Before It Spots Your Teens,* is how he communicates his deep understanding of situational awareness and gives parents practical tools to help prepare their teens to be safe, alert, and engaged with their environment. What makes this book different from other situational awareness books is that Gary first acknowledges most teens' inherent sense of invulnerability and their irresistible need for attention-grabbing digital content, then offers a system to help parents keep their teens safe in this unpredictable world.

Gary has perfectly combined the situational awareness tools developed as a Federal Air Marshal with the experience of have raising his own now-adult children to help other parents raise situationally aware teenagers. To say I recommend this book for parents and teens is an understatement.

 —Joshua T. Frank, founder and president of Consequence of Habit

Gary's knowledge of and experience in situational awareness is unmatched. This third book demonstrates that yet again. I have three very special teens in my life, and I have learned over and over they have a language and lifestyle all their own. In this book, Gary tackles those challenges of communicating with teenagers and spells out wonderful and effective ways to teach them how to be aware in their specific surroundings. I love that I now have tips and tactics to make sure each of these sweet kids are safe when they are out in the world. And of course, as a bonus, I continue to build my knowledge along the way, too.

 —Andrea Barkley, firearms instructor, and retired
 Foreign Service Specialist

In this third book in his self-help series, Quesenberry draws on his years of professional training and personal experiences to help parents keep their teens safe.

The author is a retired air marshal who spent his working life training new recruits in situational awareness. In these pages, he shares his acquired wisdom and strategies with parents, so they can teach their teens to "identify and process environmental cues to accurately predict the actions of others" and keep safe accordingly. By revealing some of the tactics and behaviors of child predators, Quesenberry hopes to educate readers about the dangers that teens face online and out in the world. He explains "pre-incident indicators" that predators may use to manipulate a potential victim, and encourages kids to pay attention not just to their environment, but also to their intuition. Some sections lean more toward more traditional parenting advice, which isn't Quesenberry's area of professional expertise, although he does cite experts and includes a bibliography of sources. He's clear about which strategies he's used with his own teens, including teaching self-defense techniques and driving rules. Each chapter has a section of "practical exercises," which are designed to help parents teach their teens skills to deal with dangerous situations. Many readers will likely take issue with the physical aggressiveness of a "sneak attack" game—agreed to by parents and kids in advance—in which a parent overpowers an inattentive teen, pins them to the ground, and tickles them to teach them a lesson in situational awareness. But although this sort of role-playing seems extreme, the author also stresses the reality of attacks in which kids could find themselves unable to react defensively. Each chapter concludes with a summation of key points, which may serve as a useful refresher for those consulting the book again after an initial reading.

A thorough and well-intentioned safety guide for parents.

—KIRKUS Reviews

SPOTTING DANGER BEFORE IT SPOTS YOUR TEENS

SPOTTING DANGER BEFORE IT SPOTS YOUR TEENS

Teaching situational awareness to keep teenagers safe

GARY QUESENBERRY

Federal Air Marshal (Ret.)

YMAA Publication Center
Wolfeboro, NH

YMAA Publication Center, Inc.
PO Box 480
Wolfeboro, New Hampshire 03894
1-800-669-8892 • info@ymaa.com • www.ymaa.com

ISBN: 9781594398681 (print)
ISBN: 9781594398698 (ebook)
ISBN: 9781594398926 (hardcover)

Managing Editor: Doran Hunter
Cover design: Axie Breen
This book typeset in Sabon and Midiet

20220129

Photos by Shutterstock unless otherwise noted
Charts and graphs by the author

Publisher's Cataloging in Publication

Names: Quesenberry, Gary, author.
Title: Spotting danger before it spots your teens : developing responsible independence through sitational awareness / Gary Quesenberry.
Description: Wolfeboro, NH : YMAA Publication Center, [2022] | Includes bibliographical references and index.
Identifiers: ISBN: 9781594398681 (softcover) | 9781594398698 (ebook) | 9781594398926 (hardcover) | LCCN: 2021950217
Subjects: LCSH: Situational awareness—Safety measures—Parent participation. | Teenagers—Crimes against—Prevention. | Safety education—Parent participation. | Self-defense. | Self-protective behavior. | Self-preservation. | Self-defense—Psychological aspects. | Instinct. | Crime prevention—Psychological aspects. | Victims of crimes—Psychology. | Violence—Prevention. | BISAC: FAMILY & RELATIONSHIPS / Parenting / Parent & Adult Child. | FAMILY & RELATIONSHIPS / Life Stages / Teenagers. | HEALTH & FITNESS / Safety. | SOCIAL SCIENCE / Violence in Society. | SPORTS & RECREATION / Martial Arts / General.
Classification: LCC: BF697.5.S45 Q472 2021 | DDC: 155.9/1—dc23

For my wife
Kelly
You mean everything to me.

Contents

Foreword

by Amber Landry

I WAS A FULL-TIME HOMESCHOOLING mom to three vivacious little adventurers when the opportunity of a lifetime fell into my lap. By education, I was a registered nurse, but I had chosen to set that career aside in exchange for a lifestyle that meant training my own children—and others—to be more self-reliant. It was in the pursuit of that passion that I became connected to the team at Fieldcraft Survival. The preparedness-based training I practiced with my own children fit naturally with their vision for a family-preparedness and women's-development division within their company, of which I became the director. I found a way to maintain my role as home educator and mom while also writing course curriculums, teaching classes, and creating online content and courses to educate the general public. My role, as I like to think of it, is to transition the tactical components of preparedness into something practical, and to be honest, it's something that has been gravely needed in the self-reliance community.

In everything we taught I was determined to keep the pedagogy of preparedness focused on applicable steps and solutions. I knew that a disparity existed between theory and practice, and I was determined to walk the line between the two and help people close the gap created by overwhelm and misunderstanding. It wasn't until I found Gary's book *Spotting Danger Before It Spots Your Kids* that I found someone outside of our company whose passions and education methods aligned. Gary's clear and organized teachings, which he expounds through storytelling, exercises, and key points, render the concepts of situational awareness approachable and practical for anyone, regardless of experience level or background.

As a child raised in rural America by a mother and father whose patient and inclusive methods of parenting produced three self-sufficient and mindful children, I never saw my ability to control my own situational awareness as something atypical or outside my level of capabilities. It wasn't until I began working with teenagers through our family preparedness and self-defense courses that I began to have conversations with those teens about the root causes of their fears. The common response when asked what prompted such fears and anxieties was, "I'm just a kid, what can I do to protect myself?" The answer, as I'm sure you can guess, is "a substantial amount," and the answers are found in the well-written, clearly articulated, wisdom-inspired pages of this book. A common misconception is that broaching the subject of the very real and apparent threats that exist today in the life of teenagers will instill in them unnecessary fear, but the opposite is true. As Gary unpacks the concepts of situational awareness in a way that is tailored to fit the unique needs of teenagers living in the modern world, you will see that this education is empowering, relieving, solution oriented, and motivating on many levels.

Those with teens inclined to be independent will appreciate how Gary approaches the relationship-based nature of this book with an attitude of respect. He encourages you as the parent to completely embrace that role while also giving proper esteem to the opinions, beliefs, and personality of your teen. He recognizes as well that creating a culture of accountability within your home, where your boundaries provide a framework in which your teen can grow and thrive, is so important. You may even find that this book relieves you of the desire to hover over your teens in that it helps you to understand that the most critical role you play during these transitional years is allowing them the space to realize their full potential while also staying safe.

John Dewey says that we do not learn from experience; we learn from reflecting on experience. In reflecting on the teenage mentality in today's swiftly moving world—a world that has only accelerated since my own teenage years—I have gained insight into just how trying these years can be. I believe E. E. Cummings said it best: "It takes courage to grow up and become who you really are." While teenagers may seem downright confusing and challenging at times (or much of the time . . .), it is vital to note that these transitional years demand a lot of courage from them—courage to find their own sense of belonging in a world where they are treated like children yet expected to behave like adults. Much like my own experience of walking the line between theory and practice, these brave youths are transitioning between childhood and adulthood, and in that battle (and a battle it often is) the only weapons they bear are those we place in their capable hands.

I love how Gary and his wife chose to set left and right limits in parenting, which in and of itself is the act of recognizing, acknowledging, and closing the confusing gap in as graceful and empowering a way as I've ever seen in a book or elsewhere. As Gary asks, "What actions are we willing to accept as parents, and what parental restrictions are teens willing to live with?"

Spotting Danger Before It Spots Your Teens is such a critical book in Gary's Heads Up Series. Rather than instilling awareness in ourselves for our own protection, or learning how best to shield and empower the smallest children who rest safely within our protective boundaries, this book teaches us how to fully empower teenagers, who are no longer children but not yet adults, to take on the incredibly important role of safeguarding themselves through a realistic understanding of the world, good communication and a healthy relationship with their guardians, and a strong regard for the value of life—their life. While all these qualities are vital for their understanding of situational awareness, I also value the way these concepts contain an underlying assumption that the teenager is the capable and strong individual we know them to be—qualities I think we can all agree are grievously absent in the self-concept of many young people today.

Whether your teen is headstrong, rebellious, insecure, disconnected, or easily influenced, I encourage you to see this book through. The skills and concepts Gary teaches will extend much deeper than simply online safety and school violence prevention. Your budding and growing teenagers will find security and confidence in the modeling of such behavior, and your choosing to pick up this book is the first step. Your desire to guide your teenagers to a safe independence validates their desire to be heard, their need to be respected, and their capability to walk boldly through a world where they can look danger square in the eyes and see it for what it is.

Never doubt your role as leader and protector; you are as competent as you allow yourself to be. Train accordingly, and believe unwaveringly.

Blessings on your journey.

Amber Landry BSN, RN
Director of Family Preparedness
Fieldcraft Survival

Introduction

"When I was a boy of fourteen, my father was so ignorant
I could hardly stand to have the old man around. But when I got
to be twenty-one, I was astonished at how much the old man
had learned in seven years."

—MARK TWAIN

ONE SPRING MORNING IN 2017, eighteen-year-old Emily woke up feeling adventurous. After a long winter, being outside in the warm sun and fresh air was just what she needed, so without much planning, she threw her beach bag into the trunk of her red convertible and headed out for a relaxing drive to the shore. With no specific route or schedule to adhere to, Emily took the meandering back roads that led through the quaint tree-lined neighborhoods between home and the beach. As she headed south, her thoughts drifted toward the remaining events of her senior year in high school: prom, bonfire parties, and graduation. The top was down on the old mustang, the radio was up, and the world was as it should be. Unfortunately, the world doesn't always play by our preset narratives. Sometimes other people can intervene in our plans and send things spinning in an entirely different direction, and that's exactly what Emily was about to find out.

About an hour into her drive, Emily approached a stoplight in a small town square. As she admired the old, red brick buildings and watched people strolling through the small public park, a rusted old pickup truck pulled into the left-hand turn lane beside her. She glanced at the man inside. He was alone, unsmiling, and staring back at her. Emily's intuition told her that something was wrong, something about the man just didn't feel right, but she couldn't put her finger on the reason why. Seconds at the stoplight seemed to drag on forever. Finally, the light turned green, and Emily continued along her route as the stranger in the truck turned left and disappeared from view. "That was weird," Emily thought to herself.

A few blocks further along, Emily stopped at another red light. A little disturbed by her encounter, she was now alert and much more aware of her surroundings. As she waited for the light to turn, she checked her mirrors. A sinking feeling settled in the pit of her stomach as Emily saw the man in the truck pulling up behind her. Emily immediately experienced a flood of adrenaline. Her heart began pounding heavily in her chest, her breathing sped up, and her throat went dry. She felt as if her entire world had narrowed itself into the space of her rearview mirror. Emily's mind did everything it could to rationalize the man's sudden reappearance. Was he lost? Had he made a wrong turn? Did he work in the town? Emily knew enough about the "fight or flight" response to recognize what her body and mind were experiencing. She took four long deep breaths, holding each for a few seconds before exhaling slowly. As she regained her composure, her rational self began to speak up. "Stop trying to explain this guy's presence, calm down, and start planning!" As she pulled away, the man in the truck followed closely behind. Emily knew it was time to eliminate the possibility that this could all be a coincidence. She signaled and made the next right turn. The man in the truck did the same. She took the next left, and then one more left back onto the main road. Still, the truck followed. Now the possibility of this being a chance encounter was completely erased from her mind. "Now what?" Emily's phone was in her glove box, and she didn't want to make any unnecessary stops. "How do I get this guy to stop following me?" She was unfamiliar with the area and had no idea where the nearest police station could be. She saw that there were plenty of houses and people in the area, so she devised a hasty plan of action.

Emily scanned the nearby homes and spotted one with two cars in the driveway. Emily learned long ago that you could tell a lot about a family by looking at their vehicle. Stickers on the back bumper informed her that they were the proud grandparents of a local honor student. They were also dog owners, a German shepherd. "Perfect!" As Emily pulled into the driveway, the observant homeowners came outside to meet their unexpected visitor. Emily quickly explained what was happening with the man in the truck and that she felt afraid for her safety. The elderly wife embraced Emily as if she was a relative, and they invited her inside. All three stood by the large front window, watching the man in the truck intently. Knowing that he had been spotted, the stranger eventually pulled away and drove out of sight. After a sufficient amount of time had passed, Emily thanked the couple for their help and returned to her car. She immediately retrieved her cellphone from the glove box and called her dad. She told him what had happened and that she was heading straight back home. "Keep me on speaker and head directly to the interstate," Dad told her. Less than an hour later, Emily arrived back home safe and sound. Her plans for a relaxing day at the beach had been shattered, but thanks to her situational awareness and quick thinking, her physical well-being was still intact.

If you've read the first two books in my "Heads Up" situational awareness series, you may have already known that Emily is my youngest daughter. Today, Emily is twenty-two years old with a very bright future ahead of her. She's my baby, and I thank God daily that some of the lessons I had taught her about situational awareness and personal safety had actually taken hold in her teenage mind. Her plan to escape the man in the truck wasn't perfect, but it was effective. The fact that she could fight off the effects of an adrenaline dump, devise a plan, and return home safely was good enough for me.

There are no known forces on the planet that can stop a parent from worrying about their children. Worry is as natural to us as breathing. We worry when they leave for school, we worry when they go to the movies with their friends; based on the smell emanating from their room, we even worry that they may be harboring a homeless fugitive. When children are young, it's much easier for us to manage our parental anxiety. Our kids are mostly either at home or in school. We watch them as closely as we can, communicate with teachers and other parents about their well-being, and monitor the time they spend online. We form a web of protection around our young ones, hoping that nothing will slip through our defenses. If we're diligent about this, it works. But the time comes in every child's life when that parental control starts to feel oppressive. As our young children transition into their teens, their minds and bodies go through a radical transformation. Their need for independence and social standing becomes so overpowering that it forces them away from the protective boundaries we've worked so hard to establish. What we tend to view as wanton rebellion, they regard as breaking away from a tyrannical overlord. Neither of those views is one hundred percent accurate, but a failure to reach some sort of mutual agreement about their safety can be damaging to both teens and parents.

I look back on the incident with Emily and try to deconstruct the process I used to teach my children about situational awareness. Something I did had worked, but given the opposing objectives between teen independence and parental control, I felt that a more structured program geared specifically toward teens was necessary. For years I had taught situational awareness to newly hired federal air marshals. These were men and women who had chosen a dangerous career. They fully understood that their lack of attention in a foreign country could quickly get them into trouble. They had a vested interest in their own personal safety, and they took what I taught them seriously. Teens, on the other hand, are a little different. The goals and objectives of teaching situational awareness are the same, but the methods you use to get that information across changes dramatically. Teens may act as if they have everything under control and that they're perfectly capable of taking care of themselves, but I can tell you from experience that there is no set age where your children suddenly become confident, assertive, and self-sufficient. Just beneath that defiant, independent teenage spirit is a kid who's slightly confused by all the changes they're experiencing. If we allow it, that change can become one of life's greatest teachers. As parents, we need to understand that releasing some of that parental control and letting our teens experience things on their own is an important part of their identity development. As your teen begins to explore the limits of their individuality, the key to keeping them safe is to keep them tethered to reality. The world can be a very dangerous place, and we need to convey that fact, but not in a way that induces unnecessary fear. I say "unnecessary" because a little fear can be a good thing. It keeps us sharp and tests our resolve. It's the purposeful act of trying to make a child afraid that can be devastating, both mentally and physically. No parent should want their child to be crippled by fear. Personal safety isn't about being scared of what lies around the next corner. It's about confidence; confidence in the fact that if something bad were about to happen, you have the skills you need to identify the problem early, develop a plan of action, control your fear, and act upon that plan to keep yourself safe.

Before we begin, I think it's essential to have a general understanding of some of the unique threats teens face. As adults, we believe we have a good idea of what dangers await our children, but the fact of the matter is there's a vast divide between what we perceive as dangerous and what our teens are actually up against. That gap has only widened thanks to the technological advancements of the last twenty years. For instance, before the advent of the Internet and social media, teens had the opportunity to disconnect from some of the threats they faced. Like most awkward teens in the 80s, I had my fair share of tormentors, but once I was back home and in my room, I knew I was safe. I could pop in some microwave pizza rolls, the latest Guns N' Roses cassette, and everything was as it should be. My mind had the opportunity to tune out the rest of the world for a bit, which did wonders for my mental well-being. Now fast-forward to today. According to a 2017 study conducted by Common Sense Media, American children ages five to eight spend nearly three hours on their screens daily. They spend roughly four hours and forty-four minutes a day on mobile devices between the ages of eight and twelve. Once they hit their teens, that number rises to seven hours and twenty-two minutes daily. Those numbers have only increased over the last few years as newer apps, streaming services, games, and social sites are added to the mix. What effect does this have on our teens? For one, it practically eliminates the opportunity for teens to enjoy the downtime we experienced prior to the Internet. Today, if a child is being bullied at school, that follows them home. Their tormentors can now harass and upset them electronically, making it almost impossible for them to escape. It seems easy for us as adults to approach the problem from a "just turn the phone off" perspective, but that's not as easy for someone in their teens. Aside from cyberbullies, our children also face the threat of online predators, sexual exploitation, catfishing, and bribery, to name a few. We'll get deeper into all of that later on, but it all gives rise to the question, "How do we as parents tackle these problems and keep our teens safe?" The answer to that question lies in education, educating yourself about the problems that today's adolescents face, and educating your teens about the realities of predatory behavior and how it should be handled.

I am not a child psychologist or even a parenting expert. But as a retired federal air marshal and father of three, I do know a thing or two about staying safe. This is a book about situational awareness—what it is and how to teach it to your teens. That's the goal here. The program I lay out in this book is developed specifically to set parents' minds at ease and allow teens to confidently explore their independence, secure in the fact that they can spot dangerous situations before they happen and take the necessary steps to ensure their own well-being. Make no mistake: this is a group project, and both you and your teen have to be fully committed. It requires teamwork, communication, and accountability. Now let's get started.

PHASE ONE——The Parent's Guide to Teens and Situational Awareness

"We cannot always build the future for our youth,
but we can build our youth for the future."
—FRANKLIN D. ROOSEVELT

1

Awareness Basics

WHEN YOU TAKE ON THE ROLE of parent, you take on an incredible
amount of responsibility. One of those responsibilities is to thoroughly
prepare your children for some of the dangers they may face as they
transition into adulthood. We have no way of knowing what those specific dangers may be or at what point they might appear. Those things
are outside our control, but we can control the amount of information
we give our teens about predatory violence and how that material is
presented. This all starts by removing some of the misconceptions we
as adults have about crime and predatory behaviors in general. For
now, it's time to put aside any preconceived notions you may have
about who commits violent crimes and why, and focus on the basic
concepts of situational awareness that will allow you and your teen to
spot dangerous situations before they ever happen.

Our minds are filled with misconceptions, particularly in the realm
of personal defense. Many people think that by enrolling their teen in a
self-defense class or giving them a can of pepper spray to keep in their
car, they're preparing them to successfully overcome any threatening
situation. With the proper training, these things can certainly help keep
them alive in a fight, but real personal safety starts well before a threat

ever materializes. This is where situational awareness comes into play. I define situational awareness as the ability to identify and process environmental cues to accurately predict the actions of others. Being aware of your surroundings isn't an overly complicated process, but because of the perceptions some people have, they equate it to some sort of superpower reserved only for spies and secret agents. This isn't the case at all, and as you're about to learn, there are simple steps you can take right now that will dramatically improve your teen's level of situational awareness. You can take some of these steps as soon as you finish reading this chapter.

Let's start with the basics. Criminals are creatures of opportunity, and they'll do anything to avoid being caught. That's why they prey on those they consider to be unaware or unable to react quickly enough to protect themselves. This is book three in the "Heads Up" situational awareness series and I call it that for a reason. Simply lifting your head and paying attention to your surroundings changes how you are perceived by others, especially those with predatory intentions. It changes how you walk and gives you an air of confidence you just don't have when your head is buried in a cellphone. This simple action gives you a broader view of your environment and allows you more time to react should a dangerous situation present itself. From the perspective of a criminal, you now look harder to approach, so it's much more likely that they'll pass you by in search of a more vulnerable victim. Now that you have your head up and you're ready to step out into the world, you may ask yourself, "What exactly should I be looking for?" Before I answer that question, I should explain how I'll break this information down. I present the basics of awareness in two separate segments.

- Understanding the threat
- Building your situational awareness

Each segment plays a critical role in developing a well-rounded personal defense program, and I cover each of these extensively in book one of the series, *Spotting Danger Before It Spots You*. If you've followed the series up to this point, this information may seem familiar, but here I present things from a different perspective. Although the nuts and bolts of situational awareness remain the same, the lessons, examples, and practical exercises I put forth now are unique and geared toward the specific issues that teens routinely face.

1.1 How Predators Choose Their Victims

So, what should you be looking for? In the beginning, the more important question is, what are criminals looking for? To fully understand the process of situational awareness, we need to take a step back and evaluate ourselves, our movements, and how others perceive us. To do this, we need to understand what predators look for in their victims and why they choose the people they do.

We can divide predators into two categories: resource predators and process predators. Resource predators want something tangible from you, like your wallet, purse, watch, or anything they feel is valuable to them. Process predators on the other hand want nothing from you; they get off on the act of violence itself, and they can be much more dangerous people. One thing both types of predators have in common is that they always have their own best interests at heart. They don't want to get caught, and they don't want to draw unnecessary attention to themselves. Regardless of the factors that drive predatory violence, the result is always the same for the victim. The shock, emotional trauma, and physical damage of a violent attack can resonate with victims for years. For this reason, it's crucial that you have a good idea as to why you may be targeted. Predators tend to stick to a specific set of conditions when selecting their targets. Knowing how they think and what they look for is the first big step in achieving real situational awareness.

Just as criminals can be broken into two categories, they tend to view their potential victims in the same way. To them, you're either a hard target or a soft target. Someone is considered a hard target when there are obvious countermeasures in place that would deter a possible attack. They appear aware of their surroundings, carry themselves with confidence, and look like they could handle themselves in a fight. On the other hand, people are soft targets when they display none of the outward signs of awareness. They look easy to approach and ill-prepared to defend themselves. Predators prefer soft targets because they pose the least amount of danger. They carefully measure risk versus reward and will almost always take the easier path.

Predators are very good at choosing their victims. So good, in fact, that the infamous serial killer Ted Bundy once said that he could select his next victim by the tilt of her head. But what does that mean, and how do you avoid being selected? Predators choose their targets using what I call the seven-second PROD. This is the process by which criminals evaluate their potential targets and choose the one that poses the least amount of risk to them. PROD stands for Perception, Risk, Observable Value, and Defenses. We're now going to take a closer look at each of these, and at the end of each section, I will give you three things you can do right now to make yourself more of a hard target.

Perception

Another misconception we may have about personal safety is how others view us. You may see yourself as strong, confident, and assertive, but from the predator's point of view, your body language may tell a different story entirely. A 2019 study conducted by psychologists Brittany Blaskovits and Craig Bennell revealed that certain individuals exhibit vulnerability through their walking patterns and that observers select such individuals as those most likely to experience a violent encounter. Ironically, the findings also suggested that individuals with more vulnerable features in their movements were more likely to see themselves as a dominant personality rather than a submissive one. This shows that others, particularly predators, may view us much differently than we see ourselves. So how do we go about correcting this? In 1981 sociologists Betty Grayson and Morris Stein conducted a similar experiment. They set up cameras in Times Square and recorded people as they walked past. These recordings were later shown to local inmates who had been convicted of violent crimes such as murder, robbery, and assault. The inmates were asked to rate the people in the video based on their perceived level of vulnerability. Movements the inmates identified as signals of weakness were:

1. Short, shuffling strides when walking
2. Not swinging the arms in proportion with the stride
3. Exaggerated side-to-side movement when walking
4. Head facing at a downward angle when walking

The pedestrians who had these traits the inmates rated between one and three, which identified them as weak and vulnerable. Pedestrians labeled a seven or above, the inmates considered too much to handle in an altercation and were to be avoided altogether. They displayed the following characteristics:

1. Medium to long stride when walking
2. Arms swinging in proportion to their stride
3. Body movement in vertical alignment, which was viewed as a strong and determined walking pattern
4. Head level and eyes visible when walking

Since you now know what physical actions signal vulnerability, you can take steps to protect yourself by merely modifying your body language. Just changing your posture and stride can make you look more like someone who would be difficult to subdue and who would likely put up a fight if attacked—in other words, a hard target.

Three things you can do right now to change the way you are perceived:
- ✓ Minimize your distractions. Put your cellphone away, and don't use headphones when you're moving around in public spaces.
- ✓ Keep your head level and your eyes visible when walking.
- ✓ Maintain good posture and take medium to long strides. This is viewed as a strong and determined walking pattern.

Now let's take a little test. Looking at things from the perspective of a predator, which of the two people below do you perceive to be a softer target? Why?

If you picked the man on the right, nice job! Based on his general posture and awareness, he can be perceived as less of a threat to an attacker.

Risk

Predators go through the process of target selection and attack planning to ensure success while minimizing risk to themselves. If they feel they can confront you with minimal danger, they are more likely to act. Some of the things criminals look for when measuring risk are simple enough: Are you with a group of friends? Do you look like the type of person who would fight back or cause a scene? Are you alert and moving with a purpose, or are you distracted? Some signals are more subtle; someone who frequently avoids eye contact, for instance, would be viewed as timid and therefore pose little or no risk to the attacker. That may seem inconsequential to you, but to a criminal, it could be the deciding factor.

Most criminals are looking for victims who will be easy to control. Sexual predators, in particular, look for people they can easily overpower as a means of avoiding risk. Todd Burke, a criminologist at Radford University in Virginia, says, "The rapist is going to go after somebody who's not paying attention, who looks like they're not going to put up a fight, who's in a location that's going to make this more convenient." In *Predators: Who They Are and How to Stop Them* by Gregory M. Cooper, Michael R. King, and Thomas McHoes, a convicted sex offender who raped seventy-five women across eleven states is quoted as saying, "If I had the slightest inkling that a woman wasn't someone I could easily handle, then I would pass right on by."

Risk or even the perception of risk is something that most predators will go out of their way to avoid, so take a look at your current situation. What attributes do you possess that would pose a risk to predators? Sometimes, little things can make a big difference.

Three things you can do right now to make yourself less vulnerable to an unwanted approach:
   ✓ Know your routes and move with a purpose.
   ✓ Know your personal boundaries.
   ✓ Be willing to enforce those boundaries without guilt or apology.

Looking at things from the perspective of a predator, who poses the most risk to an attacker? Why?

The two people on the left pose more of a risk to potential attackers. Their heads are up and they're in a group. This makes them much more of a hard target than the guy on the right.

Observable Value

What do you think of when you think of value? A big house in a nice neighborhood, a sports car, or a Rolex watch? We all have an image in our mind of what real value looks like, but value is subjective, and it can look much different to you than it does to a potential attacker. The one thing that predators hold most valuable to them is their own personal safety. It has nothing to do with the car you drive or the watch you're wearing. Criminals find those things attractive, but the real value lies in what they can take from you and get away with without being caught. That's why situational awareness is the number-one deterrent to street crime. If it even remotely looks like you'll see them coming, raise an alarm, or put up a fight to protect what's yours, predators will move along to the next target. That said, sometimes the level of value you display may be worth the added risk of arrest or injury. For example, if a criminal sees someone with an expensive Louis Vuitton bag slung over their shoulder but that person is in a more crowded area or with friends, the criminal may find the increased level of risk worth the reward of getting away with an expensive bag. For that reason, it's important to be aware of what personal possessions you're showing to others. I'm not telling you what to wear or what handbag is most appropriate in public, but I will tell you that if you have anything of value on your person that's visible to other people, it's a good idea to do these three things:

Three things you can do right now to help minimize observable value:
- ✓ Minimize the visibility of valuables when you're in public.
- ✓ If it's not something worth fighting for, leave it at home.
- ✓ Maintain a safe space between you and the people around you.

Which of the pictures below best demonstrates observable value?

The person on the right is displaying more observable value. Electronic devices can be easily flipped for cash, which makes them very appealing to resource predators.

Defenses

Imagine for a moment you're a burglar casing two houses in a nice neighborhood. Both houses have well-manicured yards and give the impression that someone wealthy lives inside. You know you can find something of value in either place; the only question is which one to break into. One of the first things you may do as a criminal is walk up to the house and ring the doorbell to ensure no one is at home. Let's say when you approach the first house you notice home security stickers on the front windows and door, and the doorbell has a monitored security camera attached to it. You know right away you're being watched. When you ring the doorbell, you hear a large dog barking on the other side of the entrance. Now a voice comes over an external intercom asking who you are and what you want. Seeing these visible defenses in action, you know that whatever of value may lie inside those walls isn't worth the risk to your personal safety, so you move on. There are no security stickers at the next house, and the doorbell is broken, so you knock; no dog is barking inside, so you move around to the back door. There are no signs of security, and the rear of the house isn't visible to any of the neighbors. You've found your target. The risk to you is minimal, and whatever you may find inside will be of some value, so you break the lock and go to work.

This exact same concept applies to every person walking down the street. Suppose someone is set on taking something from you. In that case, the first thing they will do is evaluate your visible defenses and decide whether or not you have something of value or if you pose a threat to their personal safety. Regardless of the level of value you may possess, your defenses are what will serve as the deterrent to attack.

Three things you can do to immediately increase your defenses:

- ✓ Travel with a friend or a group whenever possible.
- ✓ Don't be afraid to make eye contact with the people around you. Averting your eyes from the people you find to be suspicious makes you look timid.
- ✓ Speak up. If someone you don't know approaches you, a simple "Can I help you with something?" shows that you're unafraid to engage and more likely to raise an alarm.

Which person below had the better visible defenses?

The man on the right has more visible defenses. Someone with a dog (even a small one) is much less likely to be approached by an attacker.

1.2 The Fundamentals of Situational Awareness

Now that you have a pretty good idea of how a predator targets their victims, let's move on to the fundamental elements of situational awareness. When most people think of situational awareness, they think of someone who sits with their back to the wall, continually scanning their surroundings for the least sign of danger, intently eyeballing every person who comes within twenty feet of them. But real situational awareness is something else entirely. It involves equal measures of intuition, comprehension, and planning. When employed correctly, it makes you appear more confident and assertive. It allows you to logically process what's going on around you without seeming overly paranoid, and it gives you the time to plan and act well before anyone else even knows what's going on. We'll take a closer look at these components of awareness later, but first, you need to understand the basic levels of situational awareness and how they affect your capacity to react to potential threats.

The basic levels of situational awareness are also known as Cooper's colors, and they serve as the basis for the system of awareness you are about to learn. The Cooper color code system of awareness was developed by Marine Corps Lieutenant Colonel Jeff Cooper and includes five conditions, or colors, representing a person's mental state as they go about their daily routines. The level that you find yourself in when suddenly confronted with a dangerous situation will dictate your reactions and affect your chances of a successful outcome.

- **Condition White:** In this condition, a person is entirely relaxed and unaware of what's going on around them. In most cases, condition white is reserved for when you are asleep or when you find yourself in an environment you assume to be completely free of threats, like your own home. Criminals generally target people they deem to be in condition white. If you are ever attacked while in condition white, your chances of escape are diminished because your attacker caught you off guard. Your actions at that point will be entirely reactive.
- **Condition Yellow:** This is a state of relaxed awareness. You appear to those around you to be entirely comfortable in your environment

while paying close attention to the sights and sounds around you. This condition of awareness does not constitute a state of paranoia or hypervigilance. Instead, you've simply upped your awareness to a level that would prevent you from being caught off guard.

- **Condition Orange:** At this stage, you have identified something that could be perceived as a threat, and you've narrowed your attention to that specific person or area. This is also the stage where you begin to put together plans for avoidance or escape. Once the perceived threat has passed, it's easy to transition from condition orange back to yellow.

- **Condition Red:** This is where you find yourself right before you act on your plans. In condition orange, you spotted a perceived threat and began the planning stages for an appropriate reaction. In condition red, the threat has materialized, and it's time to put those plans into action. This is where the heart rate becomes elevated, and the fight, flight, or freeze responses are triggered. Your body prepares itself for confrontation, and the adrenaline starts pumping into your system. At this point, your level of training and understanding of what is happening to you has a significant impact on the outcome.

- **Condition Black:** Condition black is much like condition white in that you do not want to find yourself there when the fight starts. Condition black is characterized by an excessively elevated heart rate (above 175 beats per minute) and a complete loss of cognitive ability. This is due to the lack of awareness and training necessary to properly deal with an active, violent threat. A person in condition black lacks the power to process the information being taken in effectively and becomes utterly useless in terms of response.

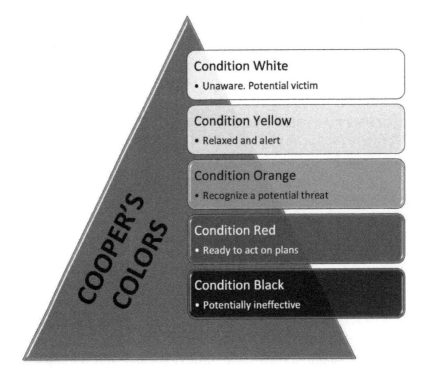

When it comes to maintaining proper situational awareness, you should always stay in condition yellow. You want to be in that casual yet observant state that allows you to take in as much information as possible without completely stressing yourself out. That brings us to the next piece of the awareness puzzle, which requires planning. Suppose you're in condition yellow and spot something you perceive as a possible threat. In that case, you have to start making plans for a reasonable response to that threat. This triggers what is known as the OODA loop.

Originally developed by Air Force fighter pilot John Boyd, the OODA loop is designed to help you quickly assess a situation and create a plan of action. The loop consists of four stages: Observe, Orient, Decide, and Act. Here's what happens in each stage of the process:

- **Observe:** You make an observation about something happening within your environment.
- **Orient:** This involves an understanding of your environmental norms to help better identify potential problems.
- **Decide:** You develop a plan of action based on information gathered during the orientation phase.
- **Act:** You put that plan into action.

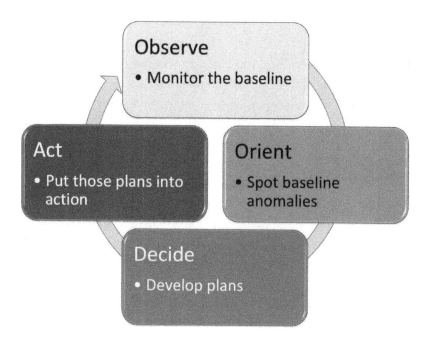

Once the OODA loop process is set into motion, the amount of time it takes for you to react to something is known as the reactionary gap. It's often said that action is quicker than reaction, but more accurately, it's unanticipated action that catches you off guard and slows down your response time. By maintaining a condition-yellow level of awareness, you're giving yourself the ability to spot potential danger from further away, which provides you with more time to plan and react appropriately. Think of it this way: you're driving down a busy highway. Both hands are on the wheel, and your head is up, eyes scanning the road in front of you. Suddenly the car ahead of you hits the brakes. You anticipated that this could happen and already have a preconditioned response to it; your foot leaves the gas pedal and starts applying pressure to the brake. You stop in plenty of time to avoid an accident. Now imagine the same scenario, but this time your head is down because your cellphone notified you of an incoming text. You glance up, and the car ahead of you is already at a complete stop. You experience a sudden adrenaline dump, panic, and slam on the breaks. This causes you to go into a skid, and you crash into the other driver. The whole incident could have been avoided if you had only been paying more attention. Paying attention to what's happening around you allows you to spot danger from further away, which gives you more time to plan and initiate a proper response. That simple concept applies to driving, walking down the street, or just sitting in a coffee shop with friends.

You never want to find yourself uttering the words, "He came out of nowhere," or "I never saw it coming." Like car accidents, predatory violence can most often be identified and avoided if you know what to look for. By understanding how predators choose their victims and familiarizing yourself with the various levels of awareness, the OODA loop, and reactionary gap, you're setting a solid foundation on which to build the rest of your personal defenses. More importantly, you have the information you need to start accessing your teen's situational awareness and building a personal defense program that they can live with. Before we do this, you'll need to better understand the specific aspects of the teenage mindset that influence the way they interpret and interact with their surroundings.

Teens in Action
Chris Ericks Saves His South Dakota Classmates from Tragedy

Years before the Columbine, Virginia Tech, or Sandy Hook school shootings, one heroic teen saved his classmates from what could have been a very tragic situation. On September 11, 1991, a seventeen-year-old gunman entered Stevens High School in Rapid City, South Dakota. He walked into the nearest classroom, demanded that the teacher leave, and held twenty-two of his fellow students hostage with a twelve-gauge sawed-off shotgun. For four hours, the students cowered while the young assailant made demands for pizza, cigarettes, one million dollars, and a helicopter over the school's intercom system. He would punctuate each demand by firing the shotgun at random objects. He shot at the chalkboard, the ceiling, and the windows. The students in the room were frozen with fear, hiding behind desks and each other hoping they would not become the gunman's next target. But one brave teen, Chris Ericks, had no intention of hiding or dying. He kept his head up and watched the shooter intently, waiting for an opportunity to take action. Eventually, the gunman placed the shotgun on a desk. That's when Ericks made his move. He lunged for the weapon. The shooter, realizing his mistake, also went for the shotgun, and the pair struggled for control. Ericks, however, won the battle and eventually overpowered the gunman. "To this day, I'm so proud of Chris Ericks for having the courage to do what he did to bring the situation to a close," police captain Christopher Grant told the *Rapid City Journal* in 2011. Chris Ericks serves as proof that no matter how bad a situation gets, keeping your head up and being aware of what's happening around you can save your life.[1]

Practical Exercise

The Pre-departure Checklist

Earlier in chapter one, I mentioned the methods predators use to select their victims. I call it the PROD: Perception, Risk, Observable Value, and Defenses. After each of these, I listed three things you can do right

---

1. Lynn Taylor Rick, "High School Standoff Remembered," *Rapid City Journal,* September 10, 2011, https://rapidcityjournal.com/news/high-school -standoff-remembered/article_07ec4dd6-db57-11e0-9e12-001cc4c03286.html.

now to ensure that you're moving confidently while maintaining your situational awareness. The next time you're out and about, I want you to take the time to review this checklist. Memorize it and make sure you incorporate each of these points into your daily routine.

✓ Minimize your distractions.
✓ Keep your head level and your eyes visible when walking.
✓ Maintain good posture and take medium to long strides.
✓ Know your routes and move with a purpose.
✓ Know your personal boundaries.
✓ Be willing to enforce those boundaries.
✓ Minimize the visibility of valuables.
✓ If it's not something worth fighting for, leave it at home.
✓ Maintain a safe space between you and the people around you.
✓ Travel with a friend or a group whenever possible.
✓ Don't be afraid to make eye contact with the people around you.
✓ Speak up.

These twelve simple steps don't require practice or training, but by implementing each prior to leaving the house, you dramatically increase your perceived defenses and lessen the chances that you will be approached or targeted by someone with bad intentions.

Key Points
- Remove any preconceived notions you may have about predatory violence.
- Situational awareness is the ability to identify and process environmental cues to accurately predict the actions of others.
- There are two types of predators:
  - Resource—Those who want something tangible from you
  - Process—Those who get off on the act of violence
- Predators view their potential targets as one of the following:
  - Hard targets
  - Soft targets

- Predators use the PROD method of evaluation to select their victims:
  - Perception: How do others view you?
  - Risk: Do you pose a threat to possible attackers?
  - Observable Value: Are you displaying outward signs of value to others?
  - Defenses: Are you displaying visible defenses against attack?
- Understand the levels of awareness:
  - Condition White: Relaxed and unaware of what's going on. If you are ever attacked while in condition white, the chances of escape are diminished because your attacker will have been able to catch you off guard.
  - Condition Yellow: The preferable level of relaxed awareness. You appear to those around you to be entirely comfortable in your environment while paying close attention to the sights and sounds that surround you. You begin taking a mental inventory of your surroundings.
  - Condition Orange: A possible threat has been identified, and you've narrowed your attention to that specific person or area. This is also the stage where you begin to put together spontaneous plans.
  - Condition Red: This is where you find yourself right before you act on your plans. In condition red, the threat has materialized, and it's time to put those plans into action. This is also where the fight, flight, or freeze responses are triggered.
  - Condition Black: Condition black is characterized by an excessively elevated heart rate (above 175 beats per minute) and a complete loss of cognitive ability. A person in condition black lacks the power to process the information being taken in effectively and becomes utterly useless in terms of response.
- Familiarize yourself with the OODA loop and how it affects your reaction time:
  - Observe: You make an observation about something happening within your environment.

- Orient: This involves an understanding of your environmental norms to help better identify potential problems.
- Decide: You develop a plan of action based on information gathered during the orientation phase.
- Act: You put that plan into action.

2

Navigating the Teenage Mind

NOW THAT OUR THREE CHILDREN are in their mid-twenties, I look back on their adolescent years and wonder, "What the hell were they thinking?" The inexplicable emotional outbursts, the unnecessary risk-taking, and the wanton rebellion are enough to make any parent throw their hands up in surrender. Even worse, trying to dissect and analyze their actions leads you nowhere. As soon as you think you have them figured out, they change direction and become something else entirely. It's maddening. But regardless of the twists, turns, and unexpected surprises you'll experience parenting teens, there's one thing you can count on unequivocally: their overpowering desire to separate themselves from the child that they were.

Teens crave independence; they want nothing more than to prove to you and everyone else that they're perfectly capable of managing their own affairs and that they can do so without your supervision. This is what we parents find so frustrating; we understand the trials that our children are going through, and we want nothing more than to help. But as adults, we look at adolescents through the filter of experience, we see the consequences of their actions before they do, and that knowledge drives us to intervene. That divergence of teen independence and parental control can sometimes create problems at home. The middle ground lies in finding the right balance between what actions you're willing to accept as a parent and what parental restrictions your teens are willing to live with. These are what I refer to as the left and right limits of parenting.

I once served as a firearms instructor in the Federal Air Marshal Service. For months we would work with candidates on the range, turning them into some of the most proficient gun handlers on the planet. Some of these candidates had little or no prior experience with a firearm, so safety was always our number one concern. When students would first show up on the range, they would receive their safety briefing; this consisted of what we called the four cardinal rules of firearms safety.

1 Treat every firearm as if it were loaded.
2. Never point your firearm at anything or anyone you do not intend to shoot.
3. Keep your finger off the trigger and outside the trigger guard until you've made the conscious decision to shoot.
4. Always be aware of your target, backstop, and beyond.

These four rules were unbreakable, and we drilled them into the students daily. They were what kept everyone alive. Once they were standing on the firing line, we introduced students to what we called the left and right limits: two very bright yellow lines painted on either side of the range. In the beginning it didn't matter if these future air marshals could accurately engage their intended targets. What mattered was that they never shot beyond the limits we had set. That took some of the pressure off of them while maintaining the other students' and instructors' safety.

My children are pretty close in age, so at one point, we had three budding adults in the house at one time. Like all parents, my wife and I struggled with ways to allow them their independence while maintaining our collective sanity. Eventually, we decided that the easiest way to go about this was to establish our own cardinal safety rules, set the left and right limits, and then turn our kids loose. Keep in mind that this wasn't something that we sat down and discussed one evening over dinner. It happened organically over time, and it's only with the benefit of hindsight that I'm able to write it down now. The four unbreakable rules of the Quesenberry household were as follows:

- **Rule #1:** Never put yourself into a situation that you can't get out of.
- **Rule #2:** Never intentionally do something you know could be harmful to yourself or others.
- **Rule #3:** Always be aware of what's happening around you. In other words, never let yourself slip into condition white when you're out in public.
- **Rule #4:** Don't be afraid to defend yourself if all other options have failed. Never allow yourself to be a victim.

The left and right limits were these:

- **Left limit:** You're becoming an adult, and we respect your independent spirit; however, your safety is ultimately our responsibility. Your mother and I will give you the space and privacy you need to do things on your own, but if at any point we feel that one of the rules is being broken or that you're doing something unsafe, we will step in.
- **Right limit:** We understand that things sometimes start off innocently enough but escalate beyond your control. If, for some reason, you find yourself in trouble, call home. We will come to get you regardless of the situation, no questions asked. We'll give things time to cool down and talk about it later.

Those were the rules we established, and for the most part, they worked. We did receive a couple of those "I'm in trouble, please come get me" phone calls. As a parent, those moments are always gut wrenching, but in the end, our teens made it through to adulthood relatively unscathed. I'm not saying that this is the way every parent should handle raising a teen, but it's the way we did it, and it served us well.

Ultimately, every parent dictates their specific house rules, but I think we can all agree on one thing: our children's safety and security is priority number one. In 2020, the World Health Organization conducted a study that concluded that violence against teens is a global public health problem. Violence ranged from acts of bullying and physical fighting to more severe crimes such as sexual assault and homicide. Worldwide, an estimated two hundred thousand homicides occur among young people between the ages of ten and twenty-five annually, making it the fourth leading cause of death for people in that age group. Sexual violence also affects a significant proportion of our youth. It is estimated that one in eight young people have reported some form of sexual abuse. Physical fighting and bullying are even more common. The study shows that an average of 42 percent of boys and 37 percent of girls were exposed to what they considered excessive bullying, and that's only the numbers reported. Today's young people face a staggering number of challenges. As parents, it's up to us to educate ourselves about these challenges and prepare our teens for some of the dangers they may face as they travel the road to adulthood. To do this, we also need to be aware of some of the adolescent behaviors that can impair their good judgment and open them up to predatory targeting.

2.1 Identity Development

One key question at the forefront of every teenager's mind is, "Who am I?" The development of a confident and stable sense of self is one of the most important undertakings an adolescent will ever face. The teenage years are usually the first time a young person begins thinking about how their identity affects their life and social standing. This often results in teens becoming overly self-conscious and unsure of where they fit among their peers. As we discussed in chapter one, the way teens are viewed by others plays an integral part in their personal safety. A lack of confidence changes the way they move and act, which can spell disaster when viewed by someone with predatory intentions.

Teens begin to develop their identities by trying out different roles and attitudes in various settings. Many of these will take place at home, while others will occur at school and in social settings, far from the prying eyes of parents. This affords young people the opportunity to explore their own values, beliefs, ethics, and morality, but it can also cause a lot of confusion among adults. The frequent changes in attitude and behavior can be baffling, but rest assured, it's going to happen whether you understand it or not. What's important is that we parents keep the left and right limits in mind when dealing with these adjustments.

It's not always easy, but by allowing your teen the space they need to work through some of these changes, you're fostering the sense of confidence they'll need to develop strong, positive identities of their own. Although we need to give our adolescents the room they need to grow, we also need to be aware of some of the common behaviors teens display as they struggle with their identity and how these behaviors can affect their safety. Dr. Les Parrott, a professor of psychology at Northwest University, lists the five most common ways teens may display issues with identity development:

- **Seeking status symbols:** This includes clothing and possessions to create a sense of positive affiliation. Remember the PROD. This behavior can also lead them to display more observable value and make them more likely to be targeted by criminals.
- **Forbidden "grown-up" behaviors:** Some teens believe that appearing mature will bring acceptance, so they begin engaging in behaviors such as drinking, drugs, and sexual activity. All of these actions can lead to more bad decisions and put your teen in a position where they are more likely to be the victim of an assault.
- **Rebellion:** Many teens engage in rebellious behavior to show that they are different from their parents and to be accepted by their peers. We'll discuss more about this later.
- **Idols:** Some teens may identify with someone famous and try to emulate that person. As a result, they lose hold of their own identity. This creates a lack of confidence and changes the way others perceive them.
- **Cliques:** Teens who are forming their identity will often form cliques because they do not want to be associated with anyone with

undesirable characteristics. Sometimes this isn't necessarily a bad thing, but keep an eye on the people your teen associates with and what behaviors they're engaging in.

Now that you have a pretty good idea of what teen identity development is and what role it plays in their personal safety, it's time to address some of the other issues that affect adolescent well-being, such as rebellion, risk-taking, attention span, and groupthink.

2.2 Rebellion and Risk-taking

A few years ago, I took a break from training with a few of my coworkers, and the topic of children came up. We all had daughters of different ages. My two girls were only twelve and ten at the time and perfect little angels in my eyes. (You still are, girls.) One of my fellow air marshals was discussing his fifteen-year-old and the chaos she was causing at home. He said she had always been a little headstrong, but her recent actions were bordering on open rebellion. About that time, one of the older supervisors walked in on the conversation. His daughters were both in their late twenties and married, so he could sympathize with the situation. He chuckled at the issues we were discussing and offered a few words of wisdom.

"Let me tell you guys something about raising daughters," he said. "When they're little, all the way up to about fifteen, they're sweet, helpful, considerate young ladies. But around fifteen or sixteen, Daddy's little girl goes on a journey. You wake up one morning, and that sweet little thing you've been raising is gone. You don't know who the hell this new person is living in your house, but she's rude, argumentative, and downright disrespectful. That doesn't mean you should be worried or upset. It just means you have to work harder as a parent. But don't worry; one day, when she's around twenty-four or so, Daddy's little girl magically reappears. That loving little angel that you've been missing so much comes back home, and when she does, she's a woman. That's when you'll understand and appreciate what she went through to get back to you."

Knowing that I had the same trials on the horizon, I took those words to heart. When my kids entered their teens, I made it a point to try to see things from their perspective. Do you want to know a little secret? I couldn't. Regardless of how hard I tried, I couldn't wrap my head around some of the things they were doing. Everything they did seemed spontaneous and illogical to me. Luckily my wife was a nurse and knew a little bit about brain chemistry and what was happening inside our children. We decided it would be better for everyone if we split our responsibilities and stuck with the things we understood. She would be responsible for the nurturing and understanding. I would be responsible for safety and security. That seemed fair enough to me, so I set about studying adolescent behaviors and developing a plan for situational awareness and personal safety that I thought my children could live with. We're going to get more into the specifics of that plan in chapter three, but here are a few things I learned along the way about teenagers, rebellion, and risk-taking.

The conventional theory on teenage rebellion was that the underde-veloped pre-frontal cortex of an adolescent creates an imbalance between the brain's decision-making center and the regions in charge of motivation and reward, which have already matured. This purported to explain why teens have poor impulse control and why they take so many unnecessary risks. But current research points out that if risky behavior in teens were simply a function of biology, then more teens would fall victim to their own poor choices. In reality, not all teens are making life-altering decisions that could risk their safety. Dr. Dan Romer, a psychologist at the University of Pennsylvania, says most teens aren't impulsive at all. He believes that a teen's choice to engage in risky behavior is driven by a desire to gain experience. To them, the risk is inconsequential. That makes a lot of sense to me. If parents continually tell their teens that they can't do certain things because they lack under-standing, why wouldn't they break away and seek that missing knowl-edge? From a safety perspective, we parents must keep an eye on the types of experience our teens are seeking to gain. Most seem pretty typi-cal and don't raise a lot of concern, but some behaviors can be danger-ous and put your child at considerable risk. According to research conducted by the Stafford Children's Hospital, some key indicators that what your teen is experiencing may be getting out of control are:

- Spending an excessive amount of time alone
- A sudden drop in school performance
- Drastic mood swings or changes in behavior
- Separation from longtime friends
- Lack of interest in hobbies or social and recreational activities
- Drug or alcohol abuse

Although you can't completely avoid teenage rebellion, you can take some steps to mitigate the risk-taking. Here are a few things you can do to prevent things from going to the extreme:

- **Set firm yet reasonable rules:** For instance, allow your teenager's friends to come over for video games and pizza. But set a rule that they clean their room after the friends leave. Make rules that are win-win, rules that respect the teen's newfound independence yet allow you to prevent things from getting out of control.

- **Have conversations instead of arguments:** Implement a rule by striking up a conversation and not by dictating one. Make rules that do not bind the teen so much that they feel pressed into testing harsh limits.
- **Have reasonable consequences:** If the teen breaks the rule, then they must have a penalty. For example, if the teen does not clean up their room after playing video games with their friends, they don't go out next weekend. Discuss reasonable consequences with your teen so that you can both have some peace of mind.
- **Praise good behavior:** Appreciate the moments when the teen does something right. For instance, say something positive when the teen cleans their room independently without being told. Compliment them and show that you genuinely appreciate their efforts.
- **Give your teen space and privacy:** It is okay for teens to spend time on the phone with their friends and extra time with them after school. If your teen follows all the other rules, then it is okay for them to have time for themselves.
- **Share knowledge and resources:** Tell teens how getting rebellious due to peer pressure can have adverse consequences. Acquaint them with the dangers of underage alcohol and tobacco usage. Explain to them how such things are not worth fighting with parents. Give the teen resources to decline offers to smoke or drink. These things help to resist peer pressure.
- **Most important is to take time to listen to your teen and hear their perspective:** They will be more likely to listen to you if they feel that you appreciate their views.

In the end, what's important is that we give our teens the space they need to explore their individuality while setting reasonable boundaries and monitoring their behavior for signs of danger. When it comes to situational awareness and personal safety, we have to discuss our teens' issues and how to best address those concerns without seeming overbearing or oppressive. When doing this, we need to break information down into manageable chunks that can be easily retained and implemented into their ever-changing lifestyles. That brings us to our next topic, the teenage attention span.

2.3 Attention Span

We've all been there; you sit your teen down for a serious conversation about one topic or another. The cellphones are put away, and there are no other distractions in the room. You get about ten seconds into what you have to say, and BAM . . . Your teen's eyes begin to glaze over, they can't seem to sit still, and it looks like it's taking serious physical effort for them not to just get up and walk away. You've lost their attention, and you practically have to force them back into the topic of discussion. It's infuriating! Why is it that young people seem so distracted? Why can't they just pay attention?

In 2015, Microsoft released a study claiming that the average human attention span had dropped to eight seconds, down from twelve in the year 2000, making us officially more distracted than the common goldfish. As a parent, it's easy for us to blame technology. With the constant connection teens have to their phones and social media, it's hard for adults to compete. But let's be honest with ourselves: are we any less distracted than our teens? When's the last time you evaluated your own attention span? I can practically guarantee that it could use a little work. The good news is that our lack of focus isn't necessarily a bad thing. In fact, we're biologically hardwired to experience these short flashes of intense focus followed by periods of what we consider to be distraction.

A new study by researchers from Princeton University and the University of California—Berkeley suggests that well before the invention of mobile phones, humans were a cognitively distracted species that can only focus on one thing for about a quarter-of-a-second. This inability to focus isn't a flaw but an evolutionary adaptation: being able to shift between highly focused and diffused attention gives us the ability to concentrate on one complex task while also being aware of our surroundings. Ian Fiebelkorn, one of the lead researchers on the project, stated that "attention is fluid, and you want it to be fluid. You don't want to be over-locked on anything. It seems like it's an evolutionary advantage to have these windows of opportunity where you're checking in with your environment."

When you put this in the context of personal safety, it makes perfect sense. "Scanning" requires that your attention be spread across your entire environment. Once something within your field of view catches your attention, you focus on it, make a decision about whether or not it affects your safety, and then move on. We're going to cover more about this in chapter three, but for now, it's important that you understand how focusing on one particular thing for too long can have damaging consequences to your well-being. In the air marshal service, we called this "focus lock," and it was to be avoided at all costs.

Focus lock is a form of distraction that is so engaging that it focuses all of our awareness on one thing and, by default, blocks out all other environmental stimuli. I use to see the effects of focus lock all the time while transiting through airports. Adults and teens alike get so focused on their smartphones that they walk into glass doors, fall down escalators, or become completely separated from their group. If you let it, focus lock can rob you of your situational awareness in times and places where it's often needed most. That's why it's crucial that we teach our teens the importance of avoiding distractions when they're out in public. Here are a few tips and techniques you can pass along to your teens to ensure that they're avoiding focus lock and maintaining sound situational awareness:

- Know where you're headed and move with a purpose.
- Keep your cellphone in your pocket and out of sight when moving through public areas.
- If the need arises to make a call or send a text, move to a less crowded area, place your back against a wall and keep it brief. If you're with a friend, have them keep an eye out for you while you're on your phone.
- Avoid using your headphones when you're out and about. If you have to have them on, keep the volume low enough so that you can still hear what's happening around you.
- Don't get drawn into random conversations with strangers.
- Take the time to pause and reevaluate your surroundings every few minutes.

Remember, your teen's lack of attention isn't necessarily a bad thing. Make sure they understand the importance of knowing what's happening around them. Use what you've learned in chapter one to have an honest discussion about how predators choose their victims and how their lack of attention could make them vulnerable to attack.

2.4 Groupthink

We all know that teens act much differently around their friends than they do at home, but a recent study conducted by psychologists at Temple University reveals that teens are far more likely to participate in high-risk behaviors when they find themselves in social settings. In the study, teens played a video game in which they drove a car. As they approached a busy intersection, they had to decide whether to stop or speed through the oncoming traffic. When teenagers knew their friends were watching, they were twice as likely to blast right through. To them, the risk of injury was justified by the positive reaction they received from their peer group. Psychology professor Jason Chein, who helped run the experiment, noted that teens acted this way even though they didn't communicate with each other while making the decision. "Simply the awareness that you were being observed by peers, if you were an adolescent, influenced decisions about risk," Chein said.

When it comes to raising teenagers, one of the most important yet overlooked aspects of groupthink is personal responsibility. Teens tend to believe that because risky behaviors like underage drinking or shop-lifting are dispersed among a group, they're no longer responsible for the outcome of their collective action. The pressure they would typi-cally feel from the moral code instilled by their parents becomes diluted by the presence of friends. You know this as peer pressure, and it moti-vates teens to behave in ways that would normally be unheard of when they're alone or with family.

Knowing the dangers of groupthink, parents need to take extra care to educate their teens about how risk-taking affects their well-being. Not only do they face the possibility of arrest, injury, or death from the behavior itself, they're also much more likely to find themselves in situations where someone with no vested interest in their safety takes control. This is never a good thing. Teens need to recognize that you give them the freedom to explore their individuality, with the understanding that they have to be responsible for their own actions and their own safety. Remember the left and right limits. Parents can and should respect their teen's independent spirit, but if at any point you feel that they're doing something illegal or unsafe, you need to step in.

Teens in Action

New Jersey Teens Save Children from Frozen Pond

Just as groupthink and risk-taking can be detrimental to your teen's safety, it can also drive them to heroic action given the right group of friends. Take for instance, five teenage boys who were hailed as heroes after they saved two younger children from falling into an icy pond while snow sledding. The group of high school freshmen, Tyler Armagan, Ryan Day, Joseph Dietrich, Kieran Foley, and Drew Scalice, were getting ready to head home from sledding at the Beacon Hill Country Club in Middletown, New Jersey. As they were leaving, they heard a commotion and realized that two small children were headed straight into a pond at the bottom of a hill. Eight-year-old Olivia Heid and her little brother, four-year-old R.J., were moving uncontrollably down the hill as their dad was yelling for them to jump off the sled. "They just went so fast right down the hill," Kieran said, "and because they were facing backward, they really didn't see it coming." The boys, all members of the same Boy Scout troop, quickly sprang into action to get the two children out. Kieran was into the water first, and the boys formed a human chain to get the children out quickly. "I knew it wasn't that deep, the water, so I just picked them up and brought them to the side of the pond to get them as warm as possible," Kieran said. The boys then sat with the children and their father as they waited for paramedics to arrive. "All I can remember is seeing the kids come down," Drew said. "When we went to the car, they started to cry . . . but Ryan was trying to calm the kids down, asking them what they wanted for Christmas, all that type of stuff." The parents of the rescued children, Richard

Heid and Stephanie Irlbeck, told reporters, "I'm grateful that it's a good, positive impact on everyone's life and the kids were safe, and no one got hurt."[1]

This is a perfect example of how group behaviors can be very positive under the right circumstances. Not all peer groups lead down troubled roads. As parents, we must familiarize ourselves with the people our teens associate with and foster those relationships that we see having a positive effect on their actions.

Practical Exercise

Setting Your Rules and Limits

Earlier in this chapter, I mentioned the four cardinal rules of safety and the left and right limits my family and I established. These were put in place to set the safety standards we expected our teens to operate within while allowing them the freedom to explore their own identities. The four unbreakable rules of the Quesenberry household were as follows:

- **Rule #1:** Never put yourself into a situation that you can't get out of.
- **Rule #2:** Never intentionally do something you know could be harmful to yourself or others.
- **Rule #3:** Always be aware of what's happening around you. In other words, never let yourself slip into condition white when you're out in public.
- **Rule #4:** Don't be afraid to defend yourself if all other options have failed. Never allow yourself to be a victim.

---

1. "New Jersey Teens Save Children Who Fell into Frozen Pond While Sledding," *Fox News,* December 20, 2020, https://www.foxnews.com/us/new-jersey -teens-save-children-frozen-pond-sledding.

The left and right limits were this:

- **Left Limit:** You're becoming an adult, and we respect your independent spirit. However, your safety is ultimately our responsibility. Your mother and I will give you the space and privacy you need to do things on your own, but if at any point we feel that one of the rules are being broken or that you're doing something unsafe, we will step in.
- **Right Limit:** We understand that things sometimes start off innocently enough but escalate beyond your control. If, for some reason, you find yourself in trouble, call home. We will come to get you regardless of the situation, no questions asked. We'll talk about it when you're ready.

Now it's time to take a hard look at your own standards for safety and develop your own set of rules. Sit down with your teen and have an open discussion about the limits you intend to set and how those limits will be implemented.

- Set the rules that you all agree can never be broken. There doesn't have to be just four; every family is different, so set as many or as few rules as you like; just make sure they're all mutually agreeable. These rules should be explicitly geared toward managing your teen's safety when you're not around. Feel free to use the ones I've listed above.
- After you've established your four cardinal safety rules, set the left and right limits. These are mutual agreements that dictate at which point parental intervention will take place. Again, there can be more than two.

Once the rules are agreed upon, you need to revisit them often, not only to ensure your teen is living within the boundaries you've set but to make sure all the bases were covered and nothing new needs to be added or deleted.

Key Points

- Teens crave independence; they want nothing more than to prove to you and everyone else that they're perfectly capable of managing their own affairs.
- Allow your teen the freedom they need to explore their individuality but set mutually agreeable family rules for safety.
- Agree upon the limits of behavior that would require parental intervention.
- The teenage years are usually the first time a young person begins thinking about how their identity affects their life and social standing. This often results in teens becoming overly self-conscious and unsure of where they fit among their peers.
- Keep an eye out for some of the negative ways teens display issues with identity development:
  - Seeking status symbols
  - Forbidden "grown-up" behaviors
  - Rebellion
  - Idols
  - Cliques
- Watch for key indicators that your teen's rebellious behavior may be getting out of control.
  - Spending an excessive amount of time alone
  - A sudden drop in school performance
  - Drastic mood swings or changes in behavior
  - Separation from longtime friends
  - Lack of interest in hobbies or social and recreational activities
  - Drug or alcohol abuse

Keep in mind that there are things you can do as parents to mitigate risk-taking behaviors:

- Set firm yet reasonable rules
- Have conversations instead of arguments
- Have reasonable consequences

- Praise good behavior
- Give your teen space and privacy
- Share knowledge and resources
- Most important is to take time to listen to your teen and hear their perspective

Avoid focus lock by doing the following:

- Know where you're headed and move with a purpose.
- Keep your cellphone in your pocket and out of sight when moving through public areas.
- If the need arises to make a call or send a text, move to a less crowded area, place your back against a wall, and keep it brief. If you're with a friend, have them keep an eye out for you while you're on your phone.
- Avoid using your headphones when you're out and about. If you have to have them on, keep the volume low enough so you can still hear what's happening around you.
- Don't get drawn into random conversations with strangers.
- Take the time to pause and reevaluate your surroundings every few minutes.

3

Developing a Situational Awareness Program That Teens Can Live With

GETTING YOUR TEEN to understand the importance of situational awareness can be a daunting task. When you're first starting out, trying to get them to implement these concepts into their evolving lifestyles can seem almost impossible. But regardless of all the concern around risk-taking and attention span, teens are bright, intelligent individuals. When provided with the proper amount of information and training, they're also perfectly capable of maintaining a reasonable level of personal security all on their own. Remember, their safety is ultimately your responsibility. When you communicate effectively and work together, you can rest easier knowing they have the tools they need to spot dangerous situations early, develop plans for avoidance, and put those plans into action without jeopardizing their well-being. That can be a huge relief for parents who struggle with giving their adolescent children the freedom they need to find their place in society. It can be done, but it takes patience and plenty of practice. The big question is how do parents get their teens to understand the importance of situational awareness and implement it in their personal lives. The answer to that may seem a bit unorthodox, but it's also simple and effective. You become the predator.

When my children were in their teens, I devised a devious little game called "sneak attack." The rules were simple; the kids would go about their day as if it were any other, but if I caught them in "condition white" at any point during their waking hours, I would attack. I say waking hours because teens tend to sleep a lot. Their developing bodies need longer recovery periods, so naptime was off-limits, as were their rooms. But any shared family space was considered "public." In my house, you had to be switched on when you were in public. The easiest target was always my oldest daughter Elda; she's very social, so her cellphone usage was through the roof. I would often catch her texting away, eyes locked on her screen, grinning wildly at whatever clever thing was being shared. She would be completely unaware of what was happening around her. That's when I would strike! I'd snatch her cellphone from her hands, pin her to the ground, and tickle her until she couldn't take it any longer.

"Dad, stop!"

"Who got caught in condition white?"

"I did, Dad, stop! Please! It won't happen again!"

It was all in good fun. I'd eventually stop, let Elda up, and give her cellphone back. I never invaded her privacy by reading her text messages or going through her phone. Those were her things, and I respected that. In return, she respected the lesson I was trying to teach her. After several successful sneak attacks, she became keenly aware of how her lack of attention affected her personally. Soon, if she needed to text her friends for whatever reason, she would stop and place her back against the wall to keep all potential threats in front of her. Using her peripheral vision to spot anyone approaching, she would text quickly, then the phone went back into her pocket. She would always spot me standing there watching and inform me in no uncertain terms that I would not catch her in condition white again. Those were always proud Daddy moments.

This is how the game went with all of my kids: Josh would get sucked into whatever game he was playing and not see me walk into the room—sneak attack! Emily was listening to her headphones at the dinner table and didn't hear me come in—sneak attack! On and on it went until finally they all realized that the best way for them to keep me at bay was to just pay attention. They even started working together and watching each other's back whenever I was in the room. As I said, it was a devious method, but it was fun for us, and it worked. Eventually, all three kids would see and comment on things when we were outside the house. They'd watch some kid walking through the mall, headphones in, eyes glued to his phone.

"Dad, look at that! That kid has no idea what's happening right now. Someone could totally sneak attack him."

"That's right. What's that called?"

"He's in condition white."

"Very good! Let's go get a Cinnabon."

The sneak attack game I played with my kids served two different purposes. It taught them how a lack of situational awareness can affect their safety and how merely paying attention to your surroundings can serve as a deterrent to attackers. But they also learned to look at things from a different perspective. They started watching other people and evaluating their vulnerability to attack. This naturally made them more aware of their own gaps in security, and they made significant efforts to correct those deficiencies when they were out in public.

Training your children in situational awareness techniques should start taking place well before they hit their teens. As I mentioned in my second book, *Spotting Danger Before It Spots Your Kids*, the fundamental elements of awareness, such as memory, comprehension, critical thinking, and decision-making, can be easily taught and reinforced through simple games. Once those basic skill sets are in place, it becomes much easier to advance children into the more focused aspects of awareness. That's where we're going to start now. In the following sections, we're going to dive deeper into the nuanced elements of situational awareness, like how to conduct initial and detailed scans of an area and how to use that information to anticipate problems, form plans, and act should the need arise. These are the things your teen will need to understand before you allow them to strike out independently. It doesn't have to be boring or monotonous. Once they understand how awareness affects them personally (I highly recommend playing your own version of sneak attack), it's much easier for them to approach these subjects with a willingness to learn more. With that in mind, let's dive in.

3.1 Learn How People Should Act

Like it or not, we're all creatures of habit. Our lives generally get broken down into predictable patterns and actions that give us a sense of normalcy and security. We wake up, shower, dress, make coffee, kiss the kids, and off to work. Once we're in the car, we follow the same route to the office and arrive at our designated parking spot right on time. Inside the office, things are as they should be: 9:00 am meetings with the boss, emails, lunch, and then watch the clock till it's time to leave. Back home it's dinner, shower, TV, then bed, just to wake up and start the whole process over. This is a very boring example, but these mundane and predictable actions can be considered our baseline behaviors. Baseline behaviors are the actions you find to be normal in any given situation. They can apply to a person, a place, or an event. Based on these patterns, you can accurately predict how people should look and act given the circumstances. In the grocery store, you expect to see people pushing carts up and down the isles or waiting patiently in line. At the DMV, you can probably expect crowds of angry, impatient people arguing that the sixteen forms of identification they've brought with them should be enough to get their license renewed. You expect a madhouse because based on your previous experiences, you know that's how it works, and it's normal. It's crucial to our safety that we continually monitor these baseline behaviors. When someone does something that falls outside what we consider to be typical, our suspicion gets raised. At this point, we realize something is wrong and we need to take some sort of action to keep ourselves safe.

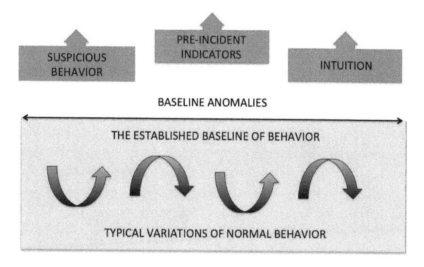

Your teen's life is no different; they fully understand how people should conduct themselves and what actions are considered normal for a given setting. We parents need to be focused on teaching our teens how to read and interpret those actions that fall outside the established baseline. That's really the heart and soul of situational awareness: the ability to read our environment, spot dangerous situations early, and make spontaneous plans for avoiding potential danger. It's not an overly complicated process, and with work, it can become second nature.

3.2 Learn to Read the Environment

There are specific steps you can take to identify potential threats in any environment. This is commonly referred to as "reading the room," and it consists of three separate phases: the general read, the initial scan, and the detailed scan. Each phase builds on the information gathered from the previous one, so it's best if you keep the sequence in order. Within each step of the process, you will be making observations that play an essential role in your personal safety. Now let's take a closer look at each step of the process.

- **The general read:** Any time you walk into a new setting, you need to ask yourself one simple question: is the feeling I get from this place good or bad? This initial step relies heavily on your intuition, and we'll get deeper into that later on. For now, you just need to listen to what your subconscious mind is telling you about the situation you're walking into. If for some reason you get a bad feeling about what's going on, it could be your mind registering threat signals that you haven't consciously recognized yet. When this happens, your best option may be to simply remove yourself from the situation.

- **The initial scan:** If everything appears to be as it should and you have a good feeling about what's happening around you, it's time to begin your initial scan. This is nothing more than a quick glance around to establish a baseline. Any time you're out in public, you will continually monitor that baseline for abnormal behaviors. This is also the point where you will begin taking note of important features within your environment: the number and location of exits, the presence of security personnel, and the whereabouts of safe spaces where you could possibly retreat in the event of an emergency. None of these actions should be overt or cause you to modify your behavioral patterns in any way. Remember, this is all taking place in condition yellow, that casual yet observant state of mind that allows you to take in as much information as possible without causing you to stand out.

- **The detailed scan:** As you move through your environment, you are continually reevaluating your circumstances and looking for actions that fall outside the established baseline. Once something catches your attention or raises your suspicion, you shift into condition orange. This is where the detailed scan begins, and you start looking for specific actions that confirm your suspicion. Those actions are referred to as pre-incident indicators.

3.3 Identify Problems

Pre-incident indicators are common patterns of behavior that criminals tend to stick to. During the detailed scan, you're recognizing and collecting behavioral cues from people in your area that may have bad intentions. It's important to focus on those behaviors that are universal and apply to everyone. They generally include the following:

- **Hidden hands:** The hands are what can kill you. Someone who is hiding their hands may also be concealing their intent to harm you.
- **Inexplicable presence:** Does the person who caught your attention have a reason for being where they are? Is their presence justified and are their actions in alignment with the baseline behaviors of that area?
- **Target glancing:** Predators like to keep an eye on their prey, but in an attempt to avoid eye contact, they will continually glance at and away from their intended victim.
- **A sudden change of movement:** If you feel you are being followed and suddenly change your direction of travel, keep an eye on the people around you. If someone inexplicably changes their direction of travel to match yours, you could be their target.
- **Inappropriate clothing:** Someone who is wearing more clothing than is appropriate may be trying to hide something.
- **Seeking a position of advantage:** Predators like to keep the upper hand. In an attempt to gain dominance, they will try to maneuver themselves into positions where they know they will have the tactical advantage. For example, an aggressor may try to back you into a corner where escape would be more difficult or purposely block an exit.
- **Impeding your movement:** If someone inexplicably blocks your movement in a particular direction, there's a pretty good chance they're trying to funnel you into a position of disadvantage.

- **Unsolicited attempts at conversation:** If someone you are unfamiliar with approaches you and makes an attempt at unwanted small talk, take a very close look at your situation. Are you in a position of disadvantage? Are there other people in the area? Has this person shown other pre-incident indicators that lead you to believe they have bad intentions? Attempts at small talk are often the predator's last move before the attack.

Aside from the pre-incident indicators listed above, there are also specific uncontrollable physiological reactions to stress that act as precursors to violent action. These are important to note because they hold true across all cultures, races, genders, and age groups. Here are a few of the more common physiological indicators.

- **Heavier than usual breathing:** When someone is under stress, their respiratory system is immediately affected. They begin to breathe more heavily or take sudden deep breaths to help distribute oxygen-rich blood to their extremities just in case they feel the need to fight or flee. Someone who intends to assault another person may appear to be breathing heavier than normal as they "psych themselves up" for the attack.
- **Appearing tense:** When we're placed under stress, our muscles naturally tense up to help protect us from injury and pain.
- **Posturing:** Frequently, people who feel threatened will naturally attempt to make themselves appear bigger. They'll puff out their chest, spread their arms, or become louder to ward off any potential threats or intimidate their intended victims.
- **Pupil dilation:** This is when a person's pupils appear larger and is often associated with fear and anger. Usually, a person's pupils are two to five millimeters in diameter, but they can dilate to as large as nine millimeters when they feel threatened. This can take place within the space of a second and is a sure-fire way to gauge a person's emotional state—but it also requires you to be dangerously close to the subject.

- **Excessive sweating:** Sweating is a natural reaction to fear and stress regardless of the outside temperature. In late 2001, onboard American Airlines flight 63 from Paris to Miami, British terrorist Richard Reid attempted to detonate explosives he had concealed in his shoe. Reid's "shoe bomb" failed to detonate because sweat had soaked through his socks and into the explosive device. His physical reactions to the stress of the situation drew the attention of other passengers, who were able to subdue him until the flight could safely land.

One of these pre-incident indicators can be easily overlooked, and two may be coincidental, but once you've noticed someone who rises above the established baseline and has exhibited at least three abnormal behaviors, it's safe to assume that you could be in danger. In law enforcement, this is known as the "Rule of Three" because it rises above the level of coincidence and into the realm of suspicious behavior. Once someone's actions meet this criterion, it's best to just remove yourself from the situation entirely.

3.4 Listen to Intuition

Fortunately for us, the most powerful tool we have for baseline observation is hardwired into our DNA. It's our intuition. What most people refer to as "a gut feeling" is actually a cognitive process. When we walk into an unfamiliar setting, our minds move faster than we can possibly control or perceive. It can tap into a vast database of previous experiences and automatically sort thousands of inputs. When it spots something it considers threatening, it will bypass the long, drawn-out process of rational thought and trigger a fear response. This happens within milliseconds, even if you haven't consciously registered the fact that you're in danger. Fear stimulates your brain and activates a release of adrenaline and other stress hormones throughout your body. This rush of adrenaline is what causes your heart to race and your breathing to quicken. It's also responsible for goosebumps, which are what make your hair stand on end. Adrenaline forces the blood from your limbs and into your core to prepare your larger muscle groups to fight or flee. This creates the tingling feeling in your extremities that most people refer to as "the chills." We often experience these subtle signals but don't recognize them for what they are: an immediate warning. Intuition is an incredible but often underutilized tool. It allows you to harness the powers of your subconscious mind to make split-second judgments that can prevent bad people from getting too close to you. No matter what's happening during your initial or detailed scans, always pay attention to your intuition. If at any point it's telling you that something is wrong, don't waste your time looking for the details. Just get out.

3.5 Know Your Options

Now the question presents itself: "I've spotted something that rises above the set baseline, and I've observed three pre-incident indicators, so what now?" That's a great question, but the answer is dependent on three factors; does the person you've identified as a potential problem have the means, intent, and opportunity to harm you? These three elements will be critical when it comes to deciding how best to respond to the problem, especially when there's no opportunities for avoidance or escape, so let's take a closer look at each.

1. **Means:** You have to ask yourself, "Does the person I perceive as a threat actually have the means to hurt me?" Most people have the means at some level: their fists, boots, or their size all serve as a means to do harm. Others may have visible weapons or at least indicate that they have weapons. After a violent encounter, you will be required to explain exactly what made you fear for your life. If you are claiming the threat was deadly, the means must be deadly as well.

2. **Intent:** To prove intent, you have to be able to show that the threat wanted to do you harm, and you must be able to articulate how you knew. A man screaming, "I'm going to punch your teeth in!"

is a pretty clear statement of intent, at least if his actions back up his words. If he then balls up his fist, aggressively moves toward you, and then draws his arm back to strike you, these are definitely corroborating actions to back up the statement of intent. Even if a person has the means to hurt you, and they've also displayed their intention to do harm, they still need the opportunity.

3. **Opportunity**: Intent and means do not matter if the threat doesn't have the direct opportunity to do you harm. If someone sends you a text and tells you they plan to come to your home next Tuesday to stab you, you can't legally take a preemptive trip to their house and kill them first. The threat has to be immediate.

If you've spotted someone who raises your suspicion and established that they have the means, the intent, and the opportunity to cause you immediate bodily harm or death, and you see a reasonable way to remove yourself from the situation, do it. It's that simple. Avoidance is the only way to keep yourself safe 100 percent of the time. If avoidance is impossible for some reason, you have three other options: escape, de-escalation, and confrontation.

Escape: When it comes to escape, space is your best friend. If complete avoidance of a situation is impossible, distance removes the attacker's opportunity to do harm. It's unrealistic to assume you can keep a safe distance from everyone all the time, and this is where situational awareness aids in the process of elimination. If you're in an area you consider safe, and you're surrounded by people you know to be friends, then there's little need to concern yourself with personal space. If, however, you're in an unfamiliar setting populated by strangers, then maintaining a safe distance is prudent and can give you valuable time to spot and react to potential danger. Aside from adhering to safe distances, several other options need to be considered when making an escape.

- Is there anything you can use to divert the attacker's attention away from you?

- Is there any way to create an obstacle between you and the attacker?
- Were there any safe spaces you spotted along your route that you could retreat to?
- Are there any items nearby you can use against the attacker to create space?

These are just a few possibilities when it comes to making a getaway. Always remember that there is no substitute for sound awareness and planning.

De-escalation: In the absence of an adequate escape route, de-escalation is the next best option. The quickest way to de-escalate a bad situation is just to give the attacker what they want, but keep in mind that this only works with a resource predator (someone who is using you to get something), and there's no guarantee of that. The other option for de-escalation is communication, but this can devolve quickly due to the overcharged emotional states that accompany confrontation, so it's important to be prepared should the situation change. Some critical factors in effective communication are:

- Speak calmly but with confidence. Confidence is key here. Never let yourself appear timid when engaging a potential attacker in conversation.
- Try to keep a safe distance, but stay close enough to build rapport or react if things turn bad—just out of hand's reach is a good rule to follow.
- Don't act scared. Acting scared or timid will only embolden an attacker and escalate the situation.
- Don't try to be intimidating. Trying to be overly intimidating toward a potential attacker will only inflame their ego and escalate the situation.
- Watch body language—yours and the assailant's. Look for changes in posture and levels of aggression. Subtle changes in body language, such as balling up fists or slightly turning their feet to get

into a "fighting stance," are good indicators that an attack is coming.

- Empathize—show some level of understanding of the attacker's situation. You may have to fake this part, but if it allows you a safe means of escape, do it.
- Allow the attacker a way out. Never corner someone when you're trying to de-escalate a situation. Allowing the other person a way out gives them an option other than fighting.

When it comes to using effective communication to de-escalate a heated argument, remembering these techniques will be your best bet and possibly the key to your survival.

Confrontation: I always keep this section of my books short. As I said in the beginning, the focus of this book is on situational awareness and ensuring your personal safety, but in the unfortunate event that escape is impossible, communication breaks down, and de-escalation is no longer an option, confrontation may be the only solution to the problem. This is a scary realization for a lot of people, especially teens. That's why I recommend seeking out competent instruction in some form of martial art. There is no one best way to defend yourself in a fight, but whatever approach you choose to take, take it wholeheartedly. If for some unfortunate reason you find yourself backed into a corner and left with no visible means of escape, there's no point in waiting for the aggressor to attack. If the standards of means, intent, and opportunity have been met, then fight as hard as you can possibly fight. Once you've created enough space to disengage, do so, remove yourself from the situation, and contact the police as quickly as possible.

3.6 Reinforcement through Visualization

Up to this point, you've developed a basic understanding of situational awareness, learned how to establish baselines, and taught to look for and identify behaviors that accompany violence. Once something rises to the level of action, you know that your options are avoidance (the most preferable option), escape, de-escalation, and confrontation. That's a pretty handy set of skills, and now that you have them, what's the best way to incorporate these methods into your teen's lifestyle? Everyone learns differently, but I've found through experience that the best way to teach and reinforce essential aspects of situational awareness is through visualization.

It's often been said that the body will not go where the mind hasn't been. This is very true, and elite coaches and athletes figured out long ago that visualization techniques can lead to better physical performance. Australian physiologist Alan Richardson scientifically proved that these techniques work. He discovered that a person who consistently visualizes a particular physical skill develops "muscle memory," which helps them when they physically engage in that activity. Richardson chose three groups of college students at random. It's important to note that none had ever practiced visualization techniques before the experiment. He then took the students to a basketball court and demonstrated how to make a free throw. The first group physically practiced making free throws every day for twenty days. The second group made free throws on the first day and the twentieth day with no practice in between. The third group made free throws on the first and twentieth day, but they also spent twenty minutes every day visualizing successfully making free throws. On the twentieth day, Richardson measured the percentage of improvement in each group. The group that practiced daily improved 24 percent. The second group, unsurprisingly, didn't improve at all. The third group, which had physically practiced the same amount as the second but added the visualization element, did 23 percent better, almost as well as the first group.

That study can help us to understand better how visualization is essential when it comes to everyday tasks, but it is also an integral part of teaching teens about situational awareness. By imagining different scenarios as they move through their environment, they better prepare themselves to act should the need arise. When my kids were young, we would continually play what I called the "what if" game. What-if games are an extremely effective way to increase situational awareness and decrease reactionary times in the event of a violent encounter. Here's how it's done.

Whenever you're out and about with your teen, whether it's a school event or a trip to the mall, take note of your position within your environment and ask specific questions about how they would react in certain situations. Start simply and then build on the scenario. You are only limited by your imagination. Here's an example.

If you're out to dinner with your teen, ask them this: What if someone enters through the back of the restaurant with a knife and begins slashing at people randomly? How would you react? Let them give their answer, then follow up with specific questions that force them to think more deeply about their surroundings.

- Is there an exit nearby you can use to get everyone to safety? If people are flooding the entrance, is there another avenue of escape? Identify as many as possible and have them mentally map out the best approach to each.
- Is there a place you can get everyone to that would provide appropriate cover or concealment? Identify as many as possible.
- If there is a break in the action, is there something nearby you could use as an improvised weapon to subdue the attacker? If not, is there an opportunity to escape? How?

Remember that it's important to have your teen think through each scenario you come up with to the most desirable conclusion, which is to escape safely. These what-if games can help you to mentally prepare for the unexpected and significantly decrease reaction times should your teen find themselves confronted with violence. The more you practice this, the more aware they will be of what's happening around them even when you're not around.

Now that you have a good understanding of what situational awareness is and how it plays into your personal security, you can begin to communicate more effectively with your teen about its role in their lives. Every year teens face violent crimes in numbers equivalent to those committed against adults and, in some cases, much higher.[1] In 2016, simple assault accounted for 26 percent of all violent crimes committed against adolescents ages twelve to fourteen, 67 percent for adolescents ages fifteen to seventeen, and 62 percent for adolescents ages eighteen to twenty. Aggravated assault was the next-most common crime committed against teens, followed by rape, sexual assault, and robbery. It's crucial that we sit our teens down and have an honest discussion about these statistics and how they factor into our safety concerns. No one likes to think that their child could possibly be a victim of a crime, but we have to prepare them. By giving them the information they need and working with them to reinforce situational awareness basics, you can rest much more comfortably knowing they have the tools they need to be responsibly independent.

Teens in Action

Devin Washington Stops a Robbery During His Job Interview

One sunny afternoon in New Orleans, eighteen-year-old Devin Washington sat down for a job interview at a local Popeye's restaurant. Devin was sitting with two managers when the cashier behind them started screaming that she was being robbed. The restaurant broke out into chaos, and Devin sprang into action. "I guess he reached his hand in the drawer, and he was trying to run to the door," Devin said. "All I could see was a woman in need of help. The only thing I remember is me getting him and putting his hand behind his back. That's all. I wasn't scared or nervous or anything like that. I just got up and did it." Washington held the robber in an arm-lock until police arrived. The would-be thief was then arrested and charged with robbery. Washington did get the job. He said he would be using the money to support his three-month-old daughter and save up

---

1. "Violent Crime Victimization," Child Trends, December 20, 2018, https://www.childtrends.org/indicators/violent-crime-victimization.

for a car. Devin then went on to say, "I was thinking like it could be my mama. It could be anybody's mama, so you have to protect somebody."

Devin's actions were spontaneous and efficient, but they were also rehearsed. Washington's football coach, Michael Franklin, says he's not surprised to hear what the defensive lineman did, because several times Washington has even jumped in to stop fights at school. Devin was aware of his surroundings and physically capable, but his practiced reactions to violent situations significantly decreased his response time and saved the day.[2]

Practical Exercise

Counting Drills

Keeping your teen alert and focused isn't always easy, but there are simple exercises you can conduct to help keep their awareness levels up. Below is a simple counting drill you can conduct with your teen any time you're out in public. These are an effective way to maintain awareness. It takes discipline and conscious effort, but after a while this technique becomes instinctive and dramatically improves their chances of spotting a bad situation early.

- When you walk into a room, make it a habit to identify all of the exits.
- Count the number of people in your area, be it a restaurant, train, or parking lot.
- When counting, make sure to look at people's hands. The hands are what can hurt you.
- When walking down the street, periodically stop at a crosswalk or storefront and take a casual look behind you. Count the number of people who appear to be paying attention to what you do.

---

2. Jason Clough, "Teen Stops Robbery During Job Interview, Lands Job," WFLA-TV, March 22, 2016, https://www.wfla.com/news/teen-stops-robber -during-interview-lands-job/.

- When you're in a parking lot, count the number of cars with people sitting in them. How many of those cars are running?

These simple counting exercises require close observation and concentration. Think back to chapter one, where we discussed how predators choose their victims. The act of counting keeps your teen's head up and moving, which makes them appear more aware and focused. This, in turn, changes the way they are perceived and makes them a less appealing target to any would-be attacker.

Key Points
- Teach your teen to establish baseline behaviors in every environment
- Learn to "read the room."
  - The general read
  - The initial scan
  - The detailed scan
- Look for pre-incident indicators that accompany violent action:
  - Hidden hands
  - Inexplicable presence
  - Target glancing
  - A sudden change of movement
  - Inappropriate clothing
  - Seeking a position of advantage
  - Impeding your movement
  - Unsolicited attempts at conversation
- Look for the physiological indicators that someone is planning to attack you:
  - Heavier than usual breathing
  - Appearing tense
  - Posturing
  - Pupil dilation
  - Excessive sweating

- Ensure that those who raise your suspicion display the means, intent, and opportunity to attack.
- Know your options when it comes to taking action:
  - Avoidance
  - Escape
  - De-escalation
  - Confrontation
- Use visualization techniques to play out solutions to various scenarios. This increases your level of awareness while decreasing reaction times should the need arise to take action.

PHASE TWO—Applying Situational Awareness to the Teenage Lifestyle

"I'm realistic enough to know that teaching teenage girls about safety isn't easy. Warnings of danger haven't become any more compelling than they were when you heard them from your parents."

—GAVIN DE BECKER

4

Understanding the Risks Teens Face

BASED ON WHAT WE'VE JUST COVERED, it's safe to say you have a pretty firm grasp on the three major components of situational awareness:

1. Establish a baseline of behavior within your given environment.
2. Spot actions that fall outside of that set baseline.
3. Develop plans for avoidance or escape based on what you see.

You can also see how issues like peer pressure, attention span, and identity development play a significant role in your teen's personal safety. These things have to be taken into account when you start your discussion on the topic of situational awareness. Trust me, there's a compromise somewhere between parental control and adolescent independence, but finding it requires open and honest communication. Once that common ground is established, it's much easier to build a program of awareness that you can both live with.

Now it's time for us to shift our focus and look at some of the more specific issues affecting teen safety. Not every concern you have about the well-being of your child should revolve around physical encounters. Your teen can be locked away in the privacy of their own room with nothing more than a cellphone and still be vulnerable to predatory attacks.

Times have changed. Few and far between are the stereotypical perverts hanging around parks and playgrounds in an attempt to lure unsuspecting children into a creepy van. Of course, these things are still a possibility, but today the world's biggest playground is virtual. Given the right access to technology, children of all ages can find themselves susceptible to unwanted advances. A 2020 survey of four thousand children between the ages of eight and thirteen found that 43 percent of those children were speaking to strangers online, with a third of them talking to strangers daily. Every year almost 10 percent of all ten to seventeen-year-olds receive sexual requests while on the Internet. One in twenty-five received an online sexual solicitation where the solicitor tried to make offline contact. Twenty-three percent of all teens surveyed experienced unwanted exposure to pornographic material.[1] These are eye-opening numbers, and the sad truth is many of these online predators are never caught or held accountable for their actions.

---

1. "Learning the Facts Is the First Step to Preventing Child Sexual Abuse," Darkness to Light, nd., https://www.d2l.org/child-sexual-abuse/statistics/.

Teens put themselves at risk every time they communicate with strangers online. Predators intentionally use the anonymity of the Internet to access sites where they can search for potential victims and avoid law enforcement scrutiny. Thanks to online profiles, predators can even sort their victims based on age, physical features, location, or interest. Suppose a predator is already communicating with an adolescent. In that case, he or she can piece together detailed information about that child's life, including the names of family members, where they go to school, or how far away they live from a particular landmark, store, or park. The predator's ultimate goal is to make their target feel safe enough with them that they agree to meet in person. This entire process is known as "grooming." It can happen quickly or over a period of time depending on the intended victim's willingness to participate. Either way, it's critical that parents understand the tactics online predators will use to manipulate their targets into a physical meeting. Here are just a few that every adult should be aware of:

- Online predators prey on teen's desire for romance and adventure.
- They develop trust and a sense of secrecy by empathizing with their target's problems and insecurities.
- They exploit natural sexual curiosities.
- They ease inhibitions by gradually introducing sex into conversations or exposing them to pornography.
- They flatter and complement their target excessively to make them feel special.
- They twist the online relationship into something romantic upon which the teen becomes dependent.
- They manipulate the target's actions to create a wedge between the teen and their parents or friends.
- They make promises of an exciting, carefree life tailored to the target's specific desires.
- They solicit nude photos of the target.

- They make threats and will often use pornography featuring their victims to blackmail them into silence.

These are devious methods, and unfortunately there's no one specific trait you can look for to spot an online predator. Mary Beth Buchanan, a former U.S. district attorney from Western Pennsylvania, said that "predators are in all professions . . . we have seen doctors, lawyers, law enforcement, and clergy. There is really no common trait. In fact, many of them are drawn to those particular professions which give them access to children."

Sometimes parents can be overwhelmed by the speed at which technology advances, but we must stay on top of the social media sites, gaming platforms, and apps our teens are using. There's a great big virtual world out there, and it's every bit as dangerous as the real one. We owe it to our children to be vigilant. So do your best to keep up.

4.1 Online Safety

I remember when my kids first got a PlayStation 3. One day I came home from work, and one of my younger children (I won't embarrass them by saying who) was sitting in front of the television playing what I thought was an innocent single-player videogame. "Dad . . . what's a finger bang?" I just stood there in complete shock. "Why in the world would you ask me something like that?" "I don't know. Someone in this game just asked me if I wanted one." I almost died tripping over the coffee table in an attempt to get to the game. My inner knuckle dragger took over, and my only instinct was to smash the bad black box! Once I calmed down, I did a little investigating and came to the stark realization that the world of video games had made a major technological leap, and I was way behind. "Well, Dad . . . what's a finger bang?" "Honey, go talk to your mother while I figure this thing out."

According to internetsafety101.org, communication is the key when it comes to protecting teens from online predators. One way to keep children safe is to supervise their online activities or limit their access to sites that can facilitate interaction with people they don't know. If you allow your teen's access to these sites, you should discuss Internet safety as often as possible, monitor their Internet use, ask them questions about the sites they visit, and research any online profiles they may have posted. This isn't an unreasonable precaution. Based on what you've just learned about online grooming, parents need to pay close attention to what their kids are doing and ask specific questions about who they're interacting with. Avoid overreacting if your teen has been talking to people they don't know or if they admit they've come across strangers soliciting personal information. If they have, ask them the following questions:

- Has this person tried to befriend you? If so, how?
- Have they tried to talk to you about sex?
- Have they asked you for personal information?
- Have they asked you for pictures or sent you pictures?
- Have they said anything to make you feel uncomfortable?
- Have they offered to send you gifts or asked if they could meet you in person?

If your teen seems closed off or doesn't want to discuss these issues with you, you need to start looking for warning signs that your teen may be participating in inappropriate online activity or that some form of online exploitation is taking place. These can include any number of uncharacteristic actions, but here are a few common ones you should be aware of:

- Becoming secretive about online activities
- Becoming obsessive about being online
- Getting angry when they can't get online
- Receiving phone calls from people you do not know or making calls to numbers you do not recognize
- Receiving gifts, mail, or packages from someone you do not know
- Withdrawing from family and friends

- Hiding screens or turning off computers when an adult enters a room

Remember, communication is the key when it comes to protecting your teen against online predators. Come into the conversation with as much information as possible and avoid becoming angry or overly dramatic. If for any reason you feel your child is in danger of online abuse or exploitation, contact your local law enforcement agency immediately.

4.2 School Violence

School violence has become a sad fact of American life. In the years following the Columbine events, there have been numerous other mass shooting incidents inside our schools. Depending on which database you look at, those numbers range from eleven occurrences well into the hundreds. It's difficult to sort through the stacks of research and statistics to pinpoint what type of violence your teen may be likely to encounter. That's dependent on factors ranging from sexual orientation and socioeconomic status to geographical region. What matters most is that we address the fact that it is happening, and it's not just gun violence.

The Centers for Disease Control and Prevention (CDC) describes school violence as violent acts that disrupt learning and have a negative effect on students, schools, and the broader community. It also isn't just limited to the confines of school property. It can occur on the way to or from school, during school-sponsored events, or on the way to or from school-sponsored events. Examples of school violence include:

- Bullying and cyberbullying
- Fighting
- The use of weapons
- Gang violence
- Sexual violence

In 2019, the CDC conducted a nationwide Youth Risk Behavior Survey, which was administered to fourteen thousand high school students across the United States. The results indicated that about one in five teens reported being bullied on school property, and more than one in twelve reported being cyberbullied in the last year. Eight percent of students surveyed had been in a physical fight on school property one or more times during the previous year. More than 7 percent had been threatened or injured with a weapon, and roughly 10 percent had not gone to school at least one day during the month before the survey was issued because they felt they would be unsafe at school or on their way home.

These numbers demonstrate the fact that many of today's youth live in fear for their safety. The best way to tackle this issue is to address it head-on with our children and give them the tools they need to take a proactive role in their own well-being. Again, this requires lots of open communication. Getting your teen to discuss the things they're afraid of can be difficult. Many adolescents (and adults for that matter) think that discussing these topics opens them up to ridicule or makes them look weak somehow. But that's not the case at all. Both teens and adults need to understand that fear is a necessary component of our built-in defenses. If we didn't experience fear, our species would probably die off fairly quickly. Fear can be useful at times. Teens need to know that they should respect their feelings of fear rather than ignore them or try to rationalize them away.

Once the topic of school violence is introduced into the conversation, teens will have strong and widely varying opinions about its causes and how it should be handled. Parents need to point out their children's role in maintaining school safety by emphasizing the following points:

- Maintain vigilance and good situational awareness.
- Follow school safety guidelines.
- Don't provide building access to strangers.
- Report strangers or suspicious activity on school grounds.
- Report threats to the school made by other students.
- Communicate any personal safety issues to school administrators.

Parents have an equal obligation to familiarize themselves with the school's emergency plans and phone numbers. These are usually included in student handbooks and posted in administrative offices. Take a few extra minutes to familiarize yourself and your teen with this information and discuss how they should handle various emergencies. If your teen has questions you can't answer, remember that it is okay to admit you don't know. Never try to make up an answer to questions about safety. A gap in your knowledge is an excellent opportunity to work together. Take advantage of that.

4.3 Exploitation

As a former federal air marshal, I've seen the effects of teen exploitation and human trafficking firsthand. My team and I have been personally involved in cases where young women were forcefully transported overseas from the United States. Fortunately, we had the training and recourses we needed to spot it and stop it. But not everyone has the benefit of that training. The question you may be asking is, "How do I, as a parent, best protect my teen from the possibility of being exploited by others?" The answer to that, as with most things, lies in education.

The International Labor Organization estimates that there are twenty-one million victims of human trafficking annually. Six million of those victims are minors.[2] In the United States alone, human trafficking earns thirty-two billion dollars annually. It's easy for us to write this problem off as something that only happens overseas or as part of the larger immigration problem, but the truth is that human trafficking is a growing problem in every part of the United States. The people who commit these crimes walk among us daily. They represent every gender, social, ethnic, and racial group we know of. Traffickers can be integrated into gangs and criminal organizations or be individuals with no affiliation with anyone. The best thing we can do as parents is to

---

2. "Forced Labor, Modern Slavery, and Human Trafficking," International Labor Organization, nd, https://www.ilo.org/global/topics/forced-labour/lang --en/index.htm.

learn to identify the common risk factors and warning signs of teen exploitation. Armed with that knowledge, we can better inform our children about these issues and how they can be avoided.

According to a report released by the Institute of Medicine and the National Research Council, a wide range of risk factors can leave a teen open to exploitation. These risks can be broken into four subgroups: individual, relationship, community, and society.

INDIVIDUAL	RELATIONSHIP	COMMUNITY	SOCIETY
History of child abuse, neglect, and mistreatment	Family conflict, disruption, dysfunction	Peer pressure	Lack of awareness of commercial exploitation and sex trafficking
Homeless, runaway, or "throwaway youth"		Social norms	Sexualization of children
LGBT youth		Social isolation	Lack of resources
History of systems involvement such as juvenile justice, child welfare		Gang involvement	
Discrimination		Under-resourced schools, neighborhoods, communities	

It's important that we acquaint ourselves with these issues to better identify the warning signs that our teens are being exploited or taken advantage of. Some of those signs may include:

- Going missing for periods of time or regularly returning home late
- Skipping school or being disruptive in class
- Associating with unknown adults
- Appearing with unexplained gifts or possessions that can't be accounted for
- Having mood swings and changes in temperament

- Using drugs or alcohol
- Displaying inappropriate sexualized behavior, such as over-familiarity with strangers, dressing in a sexualized manner, or "sexting"
- Showing signs of unexplained physical harm, such as cuts and bruising

If you witness any of these behaviors in your teen and become concerned for their safety, talk to them. This might not be easy, but they must know you care and will be there to support them.

Teens commonly face a myriad of problems that we as adults can only begin to imagine. As I mentioned earlier, the times have changed, and we have a responsibility to stay on top of the issues our children deal with. A good friend of mine, former Navy SEAL Craig "Sawman" Sawyer, started Vets 4 Child Rescue, a nonprofit organization dedicated to raising awareness about the epidemic of child trafficking and exploitation in the United States. Their website, https://www.vets4childrescue.org, is a fantastic resource for teens and parents to educate themselves on personal safety and the dangers of human trafficking. I highly recommend you take the time to sit down and explore this site with your children.

Teens in Action

Teen Who Helped Stop School Shooting Becomes a Marine

On May 7th, 2019, a Colorado teen helped tackle and disarm a gunman during a school shooting. Brendan Bialy, eighteen, helped subdue one of two shooters who entered Highlands Ranch STEM School in Denver's southern suburbs. Brendan has now recently graduated from Marine Corps basic training as a distinguished graduate. He also earned a meritorious promotion to private first class. "My thoughts on becoming a Marine were nothing but reinforced after the shooting," he said in an interview with the *Denver Post*. "What I saw that day was complete and total malevolence, bad overcome by good." While many other students ran through the halls shouting or hid during the attack, Bialy and two friends tried to tackle one of the gunmen. Bialy's friend Kendrick Castillo, eighteen, was killed in the shooting. Eight other students were injured, including Joshua Jones, who suffered two gunshot wounds as he helped tackle the gunman. Bialy, who was uninjured aside from a few cuts and scrapes, made a split-second decision to take action after seeing his friend unhesitatingly throw himself on the shooter. He later told reporters, "I don't like the idea of running and hiding." After seeing Castillo on the ground, not moving, Bialy tried to resuscitate his friend, who he'd known since freshman year. "Kendrick Castillo died a legend," Baily said. "I know he will be with me for the rest of my life." Staff Sergeant Marcus Chestnut, one of Baily's drill instructors, stated that Bialy showed qualities the Corps seeks to instill. "Quick reaction, willingness to fight . . . I don't think recruit training changed Bialy," Chestnut said. "He is who he was when he first got here. I think we just gave him some additional attributes that made him a stronger man and a basically trained Marine."[3]

Practical Exercise

The School Interview

This one is specifically for parents and caregivers. Every school has its own standards for parental involvement during emergencies. To prevent possibly risking your child or their classmates' safety, adults need to understand what the school and local law enforcement require of them during these situations.

Contact your teen's school and schedule an appointment with an administrator to discuss safety protocols and what your role would be during a crisis. The National Parent Teacher Association (PTA) recommends asking the following questions:

---

3. Chad Garland, "Teen Who Disarmed Colorado School Shooter Is Now a Marine," *Stars and Stripes,* October 4, 2019, https://www.stripes.com/news/teenager-who-disarmed-colorado-school-shooter-is-now-a-marine-1.601668.

1. Does our school have a school safety team? If so, who's on it?
2. Does our school have a current school safety policy in place? If yes,
   a. Where can I review the current policy?
   b. What is included in the policy?
   c. How often is it evaluated and updated?
3. Does your teen's school have a threat assessment protocol? If yes,
   a. What does it include?
   b. Who is responsible for conducting the threat assessment?
4. Does the school have a visitor check-in/check-out system, proper lighting, and secure access points to the school campus?
5. Does the school have a school resource officer or other types of security personnel on school premises? If yes,
   a. What type of training have they received?
   b. Is it ongoing?
   c. Are they armed?
   d. What is their role and authority in the event of an actual emergency?
6. Are school safety drills conducted throughout the school year? If so, what can students and parents expect from these drills?
7. In the event of an actual emergency, how are students evacuated from the building?
8. How are parents and students reunited?
9. What are the policies regarding bullying, harassment, and discipline?
10. What crisis response services and psychological support measures are in place in the event of an actual emergency?
11. Are there anonymous reporting and response procedures where students, staff, and families can report concerning behaviors or potential threats?
12. How are families notified if there is a school safety threat or incident?

Feel free to add as many questions to the list as you feel are necessary. Once you have the answers to your questions, it's time for another discussion. Have a family meeting to review how much your teen knows about their school's emergency plans. If you find any gaps in their knowledge of the protocols, make sure you fill them in on what's expected of them in case of an emergency.

Key Points
- Parents must understand the tactics online predators will use to manipulate their targets into a physical meeting. Online predators prey on teen's desire for romance and adventure.
  - Predators develop trust and a sense of secrecy by empathizing with their target's problems and insecurities.
  - They exploit natural sexual curiosities.
  - They ease inhibitions by gradually introducing sex into conversations or exposing them to pornography.
  - They flatter and compliment their target excessively to make them feel special.
  - They twist the online relationship into something romantic upon which the teen becomes dependent.
  - They manipulate the actions of their target to create a wedge between the teen and their parents or friends.
  - They make promises of an exciting, carefree life tailored to the target's specific desires.
  - They solicit nude photos of the target.
  - They make threats and will often use pornography featuring their victim to blackmail them into silence.
- Parents need to point out the role students have in maintaining school safety by emphasizing the following points:
  - Maintain vigilance and good situational awareness.
  - Follow school safety guidelines.
  - Don't provide building access to strangers.
  - Report strangers or suspicious activity on school grounds.

- ○ Report threats to the school made by other students.
- ○ Communicate any personal safety issues to school administrators.
- It's important that we acquaint ourselves with the warning signs that our teens are being exploited or taken advantage of. Some of those signs may include:
  - ○ Going missing for periods of time or regularly returning home late
  - ○ Skipping school or being disruptive in class
  - ○ Associating with unknown adults
  - ○ Appearing with unexplained gifts or possessions that can't be accounted for
  - ○ Having mood swings and changes in temperament
  - ○ Using drugs or alcohol
  - ○ Displaying inappropriate sexualized behavior, such as over-familiarity with strangers, dressing in a sexualized manner, or "sexting"
  - ○ Showing signs of unexplained physical harm, such as cuts and bruising

5

Pre-driver's License Teens

SO FAR, WE'VE TAKEN a comprehensive look at the basics of situational awareness and how it applies to the teenage lifestyle. We've also covered some of the unique challenges teens face both internally and from external threats. With both of those pieces in place, how do we now start the process of allowing our children to be more responsible and independent? I'll forewarn you that it's not easy and requires a lot of patience from both the parent and the teen, so buckle up.

From the time your child is born up to about eight months old, they're reasonably immobile. They have no means of getting from point A to point B on their own, so they have to be carried or pushed anywhere you want them to go. If you sit them down to do something else, it's safe to assume they'll be right where you left them when you come back. Sometime around the eight-month mark, they begin to crawl, and they get really good at it really fast. You sit your baby down, run to the fridge, and when you come back, they're gone—scooting away as fast as they can, usually laughing like a maniac. By the time they're one-year-old, they've become highly mobile, walking and running everywhere at a pretty astonishing pace. That's when things change. They become tiny little escape artists, almost impossible to keep up with, and they've developed a new determination to get their hands on every dangerous item they can find. As nerve-wracking as it can be, these are precious moments. Babies are cute, and the changes they go through in that first year are a miracle to behold. Now fast-forward twelve years. Your baby is thirteen. They may look and act much differently, but this cycle of mobility is about to repeat itself, and I can promise you, this time, it's going to be much more stressful.

My wife and I tried to stay pretty structured when it came to what we allowed our kids to do and when. "You can have your first smartphone when you're twelve. You can start dating when you're fifteen. As long as your grades are up and you're staying out of trouble, we'll start teaching you to drive, and you can get your license as soon as you turn sixteen. The amount of freedom you get after that is dependent on your grades, your attitude, and how clean your room is." We also encouraged our kids to stay active in sports and extracurricular activities. With three kids only five years apart from oldest to youngest, we stayed pretty busy. When you look at that progression from early teen to the driver's license, it's easy to see how that pattern of mobility I mentioned earlier plays out again during the teenage years. Between the ages of twelve and fifteen, our kids were mostly dependent on us or another adult to get them from place to place. When we left them somewhere, that's usually where they were when we got back. At fifteen, we started allowing them to date and go places with friends. There they'd go scooting off, laughing like maniacs again. At sixteen, they got their driver's license and were fully and independently mobile. Once again, they're hard to keep up with, and it looks like they're doing everything they can to find new ways to hurt themselves.

It's never easy for a parent to start handing over the reins of freedom to their kids, and each stage of this process comes with its own unique set of challenges. In this chapter, we're going to break down a few of those challenges and equip you with the tools you need to effectively manage the transition from a reliant child to an independent teen. As we do this, keep in mind that we're also shifting the responsibility of who's in charge of their safety. We have to do everything we can to ensure that the people they're with and the places they go are safe and appropriate. As we slowly hand over more and more control, we have to be confident that the lessons we've taught them about situational awareness and personal safety have taken hold. It's a process, and it has to happen incrementally. Let's begin by looking at some of the challenges you'll face before your teen gets their driver's license.

5.1 Home Alone

With the busy schedules we adults tend to keep, life is bound to throw us a curveball from time to time. Whether it's after-hours work obligations, an unexpected snow day, or childcare issues, there may come a time when we have to ask our children, "Are you okay to stay by yourself for a little while?" The decision to leave your kids at home by themselves depends on their age and level of maturity. I never recommend leaving children under twelve at home alone, but as they get older and start to gain confidence, there's nothing wrong with having them care for themselves once in a while.

Before you decide to leave your teen at home alone, make sure you check in with them first to see how they feel about the idea. In most cases, kids jump at the opportunity to be left to their own devices for a few hours. The chance to relax, watch whatever they want on television, and eat all the snacks they want without parental oversight is pretty appealing to a teen, but make sure they're willing to abide by a few rules before you walk out the door. According to the Children's Wellness Center (CWC) in Atlanta, Georgia, here are a few things to consider before leaving your teen home alone:

Set the Ground Rules:
- Establish clear guidelines about strangers. Let your teen/preteen know about the dangers of talking to strangers online and in-person and discuss why they should avoid situations such as

answering the door, hosting friends, or leaving the house unaccompanied.

- Set any restrictions that may be necessary on available electronics such as phones, television, tablets, and other smart devices.
- If you are leaving multiple kids home alone, designate a leader. Define written rules to help avoid conflict. Consider assigning each child a role in the emergency plan in the case of a fire, intruder, injury, or other potentially hazardous circumstance.
- Prepare emergency phone numbers, first aid kits, alarm codes, and evacuation plans. Talk about these plans and practice them multiple times in advance.
- Take a gradual approach. Leave your teen/preteen home alone for small amounts of time to slowly introduce them to the responsibilities of being on their own.
- Before you leave your child home alone for the first few times, make sure to plan ahead so you have time to prepare all the safety measures in advance.

Prepare Your Home

No matter how responsible your child is, accidents can happen. To keep your teen safe, be sure to prepare your home before leaving.

- Secure doors and windows. Ensure they are all locked when you leave and remind your child that they should always remain locked.
- If you have a home security system, make sure your teen knows how to set it once you walk out the door and what to do if the system is triggered.
- Alert neighbors or a trusted nearby emergency contact when you are traveling farther away.
- Lock away sharp objects, weapons, medicine, and other harmful or toxic products to avoid accidental harm.
- Along with these safety measures, remember to check in with your child periodically when you are away for long periods. Check-ins help to reassure you both that everything is okay.

When it came to my own children, being left at home alone was their first step toward independence. It allowed them to demonstrate that they could follow the rules and act responsibly, plus it gave my wife and me the peace of mind we needed for the big changes to come.

5.2 Malls, Movies, And Parks

It all starts with the parent drop-off. We've all been to the mall a thousand times with our children, but at some point the presence of a parent makes them feel way less cool. I know . . . how could that possibly be that case? I mean, look at you . . . you're awesome, right? I'm sure you are, but we have to come to grips with the fact that your teen may not always see it that way. I'll never forget the evening my son told me that it was no longer okay for me to kiss him goodnight.

"Dad, I'm twelve now; I'm practically a grown man."

"You're right son . . . high-five?"

"Good night, Dad."

These things happen, and although they can sting a little at the time, nothing fills a parent's heart with more pride than seeing their babies turn into little grownups.

Teens just want to exercise a little freedom, strike out on their own now and again, and hang out with their friends free from parental over-watch. This is perfectly normal and not necessarily a bad thing. By the time our kids hit their teens, we could use a little break. Today's adults have a very hectic lifestyle. In a recent study conducted by the Pew Research Center, 46 percent of American households with children between the ages of seven and eighteen have parents that both work full-time. In most cases, that's a necessity, given that in 2019 the median household income was $68,703. Now add that the estimated cost of raising a child from birth through age seventeen is $233,610 or almost $14,000 annually. If you have three children, that's eating up over half of your annual income. In other words, parents are breaking their backs to support their families, and they're exhausted. Once your child gets old enough to take a little responsibility and leave the house from time to time, you're ready. You could use the break, but now's not the time to just drop your teen off somewhere without exercising a little due diligence first. Here are a few things both you and your teen need to consider.

First, you should never leave your child unattended in a public area until you feel they are old enough and responsible enough to follow the rules, make good decisions, and exercise an appropriate level of situational awareness. On top of that, my wife and I had a rule: we never dropped our kids off with anyone we hadn't met first. It's that simple. Once we felt our kids were ready, we never minded them hanging out at the mall or the park, but we did want to know who they were hanging out with. In most cases, we met our kid's friends and their friend's parents through school events. As I mentioned earlier, we always encouraged our kids to pursue sports and other extracurricular activities. We found that in most cases, those were the kids they tended to congregate with anyway. Plus, it was an excellent opportunity for us to speak with other parents and exchange numbers with them. Once we got to know our kid's friends and their families, it was much easier for us to relinquish a little of that protective control and let them do things on their own, but that didn't come without restrictions. Here are a few of the protocols we set for unaccompanied drop-offs:

- Make sure your teen knows your phone number. This may seem a bit silly for someone in their teens, but they need to be able to recite it. All too often, people program contacts into their phones and forget the numbers. If that phone becomes lost or stolen, they may need to call you from another phone. Make sure they have emergency numbers memorized before they leave the house.
- Talk to your teen about situational awareness before you drop them off. Remind them of the pitfalls of walking around unaware. Have them talk you through the process of establishing a baseline and what predatory behaviors they should be looking out for.
- Establish strict pickup points and time. This was non-negotiable in our house. I always taught my kids that if they were early, they

were on time. If they were on time, they were late, and if they were late, they were grounded.

- If your teen will be away from the house for more than a couple of hours, establish check-in times. We always had our kids give us a call every two hours just to check in and let us know everything was okay.
- Ensure they know it's for an important reason if you call them outside the established check-in times. Always answer. If for some reason they can't answer (say they're inside a movie theatre), have them text you back right away. Again, this is non-negotiable.
- Review the safety rules you've worked together to set and go over the left and right limits again before you drop them off. It's important to let them know you respect their freedom and privacy, but that if anything happens they feel could get them into trouble, call. You'll be there to get them, no questions asked.

5.3 Sleepovers

Sleepovers are a big part of adolescent friendships nowadays. When my children were young, it felt like we were hosting sleepovers on a pretty regular basis. In the beginning, these seemed like nothing more than fun, extended play dates. The kids would stay up late and pig out on popcorn and ice cream. They watched movies and eventually fall asleep scattered all over the living room furniture. When children are young, sleepovers are coordinated, controlled, and restricted to the confines of whatever house they're staying in. Once they hit their teens, things change a bit. Now all of a sudden, it's, "We're going to hang out at the mall for a bit, then Kara's mom is picking us up, and we're going to dinner at her house; we may go see a movie, but we'll be sleeping at Hanna's place tonight." It can get a little confusing, and believe me when I tell you that this is sometimes by design. Just as we teach our children to trust their intuition, we parents have to stay in tune with those gut feelings as well. If at any point the information you're getting from your teen about where they'll be or what they'll be doing seems a bit puzzling or questionable, don't be afraid to shut it down, or at least nail down some facts.

Here are a few things you may want to clarify before letting your teen leave the house for an overnight stay.

- **Know who your teen is staying with:** If you're lucky, you've already established a relationship with most of your teen's friends and their families. This makes things much easier when it comes to managing overnight stays and keeping in touch with an adult on the receiving end. If someone new comes into the picture, make sure you know who that new friend is and what they're like. Never let your teen go off on an overnight stay with someone you haven't met.
- **Set limits:** Teenagers may think they're all grown up, but it may be necessary to remind them that they are not yet adults. It's up to the parents involved to set the rules. If you decide to allow a sleepover, make sure you articulate what you expect from your teen

in terms of where they go and how they act when they're away from home. You should also communicate with the other parents to make sure you're all on the same page when it comes to setting house rules.

- **Sleepovers are earned:** Sleepovers are a lot of fun, and they're an excellent way for your teen to experience a change of scenery. Before you agree to a sleepover, take the time to sit down with your teen and explain that the sleepover is a reward for their good behavior. It's something that has to be earned and will not be given freely in the future.

- **Give your teen a way out:** Resisting peer pressure can be a challenge. Before your teen leaves the house, make sure you discuss an escape plan so they have an excuse to leave if they begin to feel uncomfortable. A quick text, "Dad, I feel sick," is simple enough. Plus, it's a great excuse to leave without raising too many questions. Make sure they know you will have your phone with you all night should they feel the need to make an early getaway.

- **Be understanding:** I know my kids are going to read this book and call me out here. I'll admit that I was terrible at being the calm, levelheaded parent. That was usually their mom's job. The advice I give now benefits from years of reflection and hindsight. If something unexpected happens while your teen is off on a sleepover (let's say a phone call from the local police telling you to come pick up your kid), take a moment to compose yourself. As long as they're safe, there's nothing worth jeopardizing your relationship over. You may feel like they've violated your trust, but let's be honest with ourselves: we all know that this is what teens tend to do, and more than likely, we did it ourselves. Remember the left and right limits. Understand that things sometimes start off innocently enough but escalate beyond your teen's control. If you get one of those late-night phone calls, pick them up and get them home as quickly as you can. The line of questioning can wait until things have cooled down.

5.4 School Trips

School trips are a fantastic way for your teen to broaden their horizons, experience a little history, and create lasting memories with their friends. I still remember my first big school trip from middle school. We loaded up on Greyhound busses and took off to visit Monticello, Thomas Jefferson's home in Charlottesville, Virginia. I've been a history buff for as long as I can remember, so this was a real treat for me. It was a beautiful place, and I can still close my eyes and see it as vividly as if it were yesterday.

As fun and educational as school trips can be, there are still a few pitfalls that both teens and parents should be aware of. Some are common dangers associated with any form of travel, such as traffic accidents, food poisoning, or minor injuries due to trips and falls. But the biggest cause of accidents during school trips is simply poor supervision. Before sending your teen off on a school trip, make sure the following precautions have been taken:

- Talk to your teen about how you expect them to conduct themselves on the trip. Make sure you revisit the basics of situational awareness and have all the contact information they need in the event of an emergency.
- Speak with a teacher to clarify the itinerary. Know where your teen will be and when.
- Clarify pickup times and protocols, so there's no chance of your teen leaving with someone they're not supposed to.
- Have an emergency contact number so you can contact a teacher or chaperone if you're unable to reach your teen during the trip.
- If the trip includes an overnight stay, ensure that references and background checks have been conducted on all chaperones. The age and number of students present on the trip should dictate the number of chaperones. Schools should have one adult chaperone for every three to five students, especially for teens.

- Ensure that adult chaperones are equipped to handle emergencies and that someone on the trip can administer first-aid should the need arise.
- Research the places your teen will be visiting. A quick online search can give you basic crime statistics and common issues other visitors may have had in the past.

For the most part, these measures are for parental peace of mind. You want your teen to have fun and share new experiences with their friends while away from school, but you also want to rest easy knowing you did your part to voice your expectations.

5.5 Team Sports

All of my kids played sports while they were in school. Josh played football and wrestled, Elda played soccer and softball, and Emily enjoyed cheer and color guard. School sports are a great way to keep your child active and associated with like-minded teens. Plus, it's a good opportunity for parents to meet and interact with one another. There are plenty of healthy benefits to school sports, from building camaraderie and sportsmanship to battling obesity and depression. It gives teens a sense of accomplishment and structure, plus it allows them to experience and process the emotional effects of defeat. All of these are beneficial experiences, but there can be a dark side to school sports that parents aren't always aware of.

In 2011, Gerald Arthur Sandusky, a football coach at Pennsylvania State University, was arrested and charged with fifty-two counts of sexual abuse of young boys over a fifteen-year period. In 2017, Lawrence Nassar, the former USA Gymnastics national team doctor, was sentenced to sixty years in federal prison after pleading guilty to child pornography and sexual abuse charges. Although the information is limited on these types of abuse, the late Dr. Celia Brackenridge, author of *Sport, Children's Rights and Violence Prevention*, reported in 2008 that between 2 and 22 percent of children and teens were victims of sexual abuse through sport. Ninety-eight percent of these cases were perpetrated by coaches, teachers, and instructors, who were predominately male and ranged in age from sixteen to sixty-three years old.

Aside from the concerns of sexual abuse, there is also the issue of hazing during school sports. Hazing is defined as any activity expected of someone joining or participating in a group that humiliates, degrades, abuses, or endangers them regardless of a person's willingness to participate.[1] In 2000, Alfred University published a report on high school hazing. In the report, it was noted that 48 percent of students surveyed reported being subjected to activities that were considered hazing. Based on this statistic, it's projected that more than 1.5 million high school students in the United States are being subjected to some form of hazing each year. Many still believe that hazing is a harmless tradition or rite-of-passage that bonds teammates together. However, hazing activities often involve humiliation, alcohol or drug use, and inappropriate behavior. Instead of promoting team unity and respect, it destroys the victim's self-image and confidence, leaving them stressed out and anxious.

As a parent, you need to familiarize yourself with the warning signs that your teen may be the victim of a hazing ritual. These may include:

- Excessive fatigue
- Cuts, bruises, or shaving on parts of the body
- Wearing odd clothing
- Skipping classes
- Carrying unusual items
- Withdrawal from usual activities or friends
- Behavior changes such as depression or anxiety
- Not being able to sit down
- Having to perform particular tasks for others

---

1. Elizabeth J. Allan and Mary Madden, "Hazing in View: College Students at Risk," March 11, 2018, Stop Hazing, http://www.stophazing.org/wp-content/uploads/2014/06/hazing_in_view_web1.pdf.

Signs of sexual abuse often include:

- Trouble walking or sitting
- Inappropriate knowledge of sexual acts
- Making an effort to avoid specific teachers or coaches
- Refusal to change clothes in front of others
- Refusal to participate in physical activities

Although sexual assault and violent hazing cases are rare, be ready to report these incidents to school officials or the police if necessary. If you recognize any of these signs in your teen, talk to them. Ensure them that you're there to support and help them in any way possible. Your teen's safety is a team effort, so make sure they know you're both on the same team.

Teens in Action
Teen Wrestling Champ Canaan Bower Stops a Kidnapping

Local law enforcement proclaimed sixteen-year-old wrestling champion Canaan Bower a hero after he helped stop a kidnapping and assault near Las Cruces, New Mexico. Witnesses told local authorities that a man later identified as twenty-two-year-old Daniel Arroyo assaulted a woman at a gas station and attempted to kidnap her three children. The children's mother told authorities that she got off at a bus stop with her kids, ages nine, two, and one, and was waiting for an Uber driver to arrive when a man grabbed her two-year-old child and demanded the woman turn over her other children. Witnesses told authorities the man punched the woman and others who tried to intervene before the woman could break free and rush inside a nearby store with her children. Witnesses said the attacker followed her inside and continued his demands. Canaan, who was across the street filling his truck with gas, heard the screams for help and rushed across to help. Canaan's dad, Troy Bower, told the local reporters that "punches were being thrown and Canaan could hear screams of terror, so he jumped in his truck and went across the street. By the time he got there, they had gone inside, and so he got out of his truck and followed." Troy Bower added that his son told him he body-slammed the man and got him in a chokehold until deputies arrived. "You fear for your own child's safety in that situation," Troy Bower said. "You don't know if this guy's maybe got a gun or a knife—you don't know what this guy's capable of." However, he said he was confident his son could do the right thing and succeed. Canaan had recently taken first place in the Mayfield High School District Wrestling Championship. His situational awareness, athleticism, and willingness to help others played an enormous role in stopping the would-be kidnapper.[2]

Practical Exercise

Six Steps to Spotting Trouble

Now that your teen is familiar with the basic techniques and exercises used to improve awareness, it's time to put those skills to use. Any time you're out in public with your kids, have them follow these six basic steps to dramatically improve their chances of spotting trouble before it has a chance to materialize.

1. Scan the area, look at people's hands, and establish a baseline for behavior.
2. Identify exits and plan the most effective routes for escape.
3. When you enter an area, pay attention to your gut feelings. If something feels wrong or out of place, start working out a plan to leave the area if the situation turns bad.
4. Frequently monitor that baseline for changes. If someone's actions rise above the baseline, fall back to step two.

---

2. "Teen Wrestling Champ Stops Kidnapping of Children," KOB 4, March 27, 2020, https://www.kob.com/new-mexico-news/deputies-teen-wrestling-champ-stops-kidnapping-of-children/5686095/.

5. Use what-if scenarios to rehearse your reactions to threatening situations. Remember to include solutions that address all three elements of personal safety: avoidance, de-escalation, and confrontation.

6. Keep a positive mental attitude. Always see yourself succeeding.

Once your teen leaves the safety of home, situational awareness becomes their primary responsibility. The more they practice these steps, the more natural the process becomes. Over time they'll notice that they're taking in more information faster without even thinking about it.

Key Points
- Before an unaccompanied drop-off, remember the following:
  - Make sure your teen knows your phone number.
  - Talk to them about situational awareness before you drop them off. Remind them of the pitfalls of walking around unaware. Have them talk you through the process of establishing a baseline and what predatory behaviors they should be looking out for.
  - Establish strict pickup points and times.
  - If your teen will be away from the house for more than a couple of hours, establish check-in times every hour.
  - Ensure they know that it's for an important reason if you call them outside the established check-in times. Always answer. If, for some reason, they can't answer, have them text you back right away.
  - Review the safety rules you've worked together to set and go over the left and right limits again before you drop them off.
- Review the following before letting your teen leave the house for an overnight stay.
  - Know who your teen is staying with. Never let your teen go off on an overnight stay with someone you haven't met.
  - Set limits: make sure that you articulate what you expect from your teen in terms of where they go and how they act when

they're away from home. You should also communicate with the other parents to make sure you're all on the same page when it comes to setting house rules.

- o Before you agree to a sleepover, take the time to sit down with your teen and explain that the sleepover is a reward for their good behavior. It's something that has to be earned and will not be given freely in the future.

- o Before your teen leaves the house, make sure you discuss an escape plan so they have an excuse to leave if they begin to feel uncomfortable.

- o Understand that things sometimes start off innocently enough but escalate beyond your teen's control. If, for some reason, you get one of those late-night, "Mom, I'm in trouble" phone calls, pick them up and get them home as quickly as you can.

- Before sending your teen off on a school trip, make sure the following precautions have been taken:

- o Talk to your teen about how you expect them to conduct themselves on the trip. Make sure you revisit the basics of situational awareness and that they have all the contact information they need in the event of an emergency.

- o Speak with a teacher to clarify the itinerary. Know where your teen will be and when.

- o Clarify pickup times and protocols so there's no chance of your teen leaving with someone they're not supposed to.

- o Have an emergency contact number so you can contact a teacher or chaperone if you're unable to reach your teen during the trip.

- o If the trip includes an overnight stay, ensure that references and background checks have been conducted on all chaperones.

- o Ensure that adult chaperones are equipped to handle emergencies and that someone on the trip can administer first-aid should the need arise.

- ○ Research the places your teen will be visiting. A quick online search can give you basic crime statistics and common issues other visitors may have had in the past.
- Familiarize yourself with the warning signs of sexual abuse or hazing. These may include:
  - ○ Excessive fatigue
  - ○ Cuts, bruises, or shaving on parts of the body
  - ○ Wearing odd clothing
  - ○ Skipping classes
  - ○ Carrying unusual items
  - ○ Withdrawal for usual activities or friends
  - ○ Behavior changes such as depression or anxiety
  - ○ Not being able to sit down
  - ○ Having to perform particular tasks for others
- Signs of sexual abuse often include:
  - ○ Trouble walking or sitting
  - ○ Inappropriate knowledge of sexual acts
  - ○ Making an effort to avoid specific teachers or coaches
  - ○ Refusal to change clothes in front of others
  - ○ Refusal to participate in physical activities

6

Teens on the Move

WATCHING YOUR CHILD BUCKLE into the driver's seat and back out of the driveway for the first time is an emotional experience. A million questions flash through your mind in an instant. "Did I teach him everything he needed to know? Were the fluid levels topped off? Is there air in the spare tire? Was his phone fully charged?" The checklist running through your mind at that moment could probably rival the one NASA used for the moon landing, but if you spend too much time dwelling on it, you're going to panic, second-guess everything you've accomplished, and abort the mission altogether. Nobody gets to the moon that way.

A responsible teenager with a driver's license can be a blessing. They can help run simple errands, take their siblings to and from sports practice, and get themselves wherever they need to go. They make life easier. That's not to say there won't be a significant amount of worry that comes along with your newly minted driver. Fear is a natural part of the process and for good reason. According to the Insurance Institute for Highway Safety, teen drivers ages sixteen to nineteen are nearly three times more likely than drivers aged twenty and older to be in a fatal crash. The chief reason for adolescents' poor safety record is their lack of experience in reacting appropriately to hazardous situations such as merging onto busy highways, making left-hand turns at a crowded intersection, or driving in poor weather conditions.[1] Additionally, teens may not have fully developed some of the physical coordination required to drive safely. Teens are more easily distracted than older drivers and more likely to speed, tailgate, text, and make bad decisions resulting in an accident.

Although threats to their safety can come from any direction, teens are most at risk of serious bodily injury once they get behind the wheel of a car. Luckily for parents, there's a reasonable transition period between the hustle and bustle of teen drop-offs and becoming an officially licensed driver, the learner's permit, or the Graduated Driver Licensing (GDL) program. These state-mandated programs allow

---

1. Behind the Wheel: How to Help Your Teen Become a Safe Driver," American Academy of Pediatrics, February 13, 2017, https://www.healthy children.org/English/ages-stages/teen/safety/Pages/Behind-the-Wheel-Helping -Teens-Become-Safe-Drivers.aspx.

young drivers to safely gain driving experience before obtaining full driving privileges and usually include three stages:

- **Learner stage:** supervised driving, cumulating with a driving test
- **Intermediate stage:** limiting unsupervised driving in high-risk situations, such as driving at night and driving with other underage passengers
- **Full privilege stage:** a standard driver's license

That gradual process of handing over responsibility is no different than the approaches we've covered in previous chapters. Whether it's allowing your teen to hang out with friends after school, sleepover at someone else's house, or drive the family sedan, that transfer of power works best when it happens in stages. Those transition periods are critical points in a teen's life and an excellent opportunity for them to gain needed experience under an adult's supervision. It also gives you the perfect platform to stress the critical role situational awareness plays in their general well-being, both on and off the road.

6.1 Driver's Safety

Once your teen works their way through all the stages of the GDL, they're ready to hit the road. But as with any new level of responsibility, there are a few rules involved. Before you hand over the keys to the car, sit down with your teen and discuss these "rules of the road" along with the penalties that come with violating them. The rules in our house included the following:

- No driving or riding with others who are under the influence of drugs or alcohol.
- No more than two friends in the car at a time (if allowed by the license).
- No eating or drinking while driving.
- Keep the music at a low to moderate volume.
- Everyone in the vehicle must wear a seat belt at all times.

- No driving after dark.
- No driving when tired, angry, or upset.
- No driving beyond a certain distance from home without getting permission first.
- No talking on the phone or texting when the vehicle is in motion.

These are pretty standard guidelines and can serve you well when it comes to managing expectations. Now that those points have been addressed, I want you and your teen to start focusing more on the role situational awareness plays in drivers' safety. In many cases, you can examine the threats your teen may face on the road well before they get behind the wheel. We'll begin this section with driver preparation.

You would never send your child out in subfreezing temperatures without the proper amount of clothing. Likewise, you would never send your teen out in a vehicle you didn't know was in good working order and outfitted with the proper emergency equipment. Knowing how to prepare for the unexpected plays a vital role in your teen's safety. Teaching them not to panic and how to handle these situations falls directly on you.

I vividly remember teaching my kids how to change a tire. With each of them, I would inevitably be faced with the question, "Dad, can't we just Google how to do this if we ever get a flat?" The answer to that question is, yes, you can. But there are certain things you just can't learn from Google. Like how much physical pressure has to be applied to break a lug nut loose, or what it feels like to smash your cold knuckles against the wheel well as you lift your spare tire into place. These things require experience to be fully appreciated, and you don't gain that knowledge through the Internet. When it comes to preparing your teens for the things they may face on the road, make sure you're taking the time to give them the actual experience. This also applies to things other than changing a tire.

During the introduction, I told the story of my youngest daughter Emily being followed by a stranger. This may not be what pops to mind when you imagine a typical roadside emergency, but it requires mentioning.

According to Policyadvice.net, eight in ten Americans are involved in a road rage incident at least once a year. On top of that, approximately thirty roadside murders occur in the US annually due to conflicts sparked by road rage. There's no way for your teen to "experience" these things before hitting the road. Still, you can inform them about what to look out for and what actions to take should they encounter an aggressive driver on the road. Here are a few of the things I recommended to our children:

- Never return rude gestures or show anger toward the aggressor.
- If a person is displaying extreme anger, it is best to remain behind them while in traffic.
- Be mindful of potential brake checks.
- Change lanes if the aggressor is tailgating you.
- If an aggressor motions for you to pull over—don't.
- Be mindful of traffic and remain aware of your driving at all times—do not break traffic laws to avoid other drivers.

If matters begin to escalate, don't panic. Take a few deep breaths to calm down and contact law enforcement as soon as it's safe to do so.

6.2 Parties

Parties are nothing to be afraid of. In most cases, they're an excellent way for your teen to develop their confidence and social skills. Still, their attendance at parties should depend on the level of responsible decision-making they've displayed up to this point. Before you say yes or no to the question about attending parties, there are a few things you're going to want to know:

- Do we know the person hosting the party?
- Have we met their parents?
- Will their parents be home for the duration of the party?
- Will there be alcohol or drugs at the party, and what will you do if there is?

- Will that party stay in one place, or will it move from location to location? If so, what are the other locations, and who will be there?

This may feel like a torturous line of questioning, but that's not the intention. Your teen should know upfront that you need specific information before giving an answer. That's your job as a parent. Their job as a teen is to provide that information as honestly and as accurately as possible. It's a two-way conversation, and its purpose is to ensure their safety, not to make them feel like they're being grilled. If they think you're being too harsh or judgmental right upfront, it will close them off or make them feel like you don't trust them. Those aren't the reactions you want. Remember, we're trying to maintain an open relationship with our teens. We want them to see that we're capable of trust and that the trust you show them has been earned through their actions. If you do decide to let them attend the party, there are a few more things you're going to want to know:

- Will you be driving, or is someone picking you up? If so, who? (Always make sure the driver comes into your house before leaving with your teen; you always want to get a good look at that person, whether you know them or not.)
- What time does the party start?
- What time will it end?
- Establish a curfew. If the party ends at midnight, what time do you expect them to be home after?

Once that's all established and agreed upon, make sure you set up some contingency plans, so your teen has a way out of the party and a way home if they need it:

- Have a conversation with your teen about situational awareness and intuition before they leave the house. If someone at the party makes your teen feel uncomfortable, remind them that there's a reason for that and that they should always trust those gut feelings.
- Let your teen know that they can call you at any time, in any condition, if they or their friends need your help—no questions asked.

- Make sure they have all of your contact information programmed into their phone. Make sure they also have your number memorized just in case they have to call from another line.
- Give your contact details to one of your teen's friends.
- Make sure your child has enough money for an emergency taxi ride home.

This may seem a bit overwhelming, and there's nothing I can write in the pages of this book that will set your mind completely at ease. These are just simple strategies to keep your teen safe and prepared for the unexpected. I know from experience that the way your teen sees things going in their head and how they actually turn out can be two completely different things. Bad things can happen that are out of their control, but don't let that keep you from allowing them their freedom. Set limits and ground rules, make sure your teen understands the penalties associated with breaking your trust, have contingency plans in place, and be understanding if things go wrong. That's the best we can do as parents.

6.3 Dating

I'm a father of three. My son Joshua is the oldest, and I have two daughters, Elda and Emily. Dating was always a touchy subject in our house. Not because my wife and I were uncomfortable with it, but because the way I handled dating was different for my daughters than it was for my son. The rules were consistent, but I put a greater emphasis on safety when it came to the girls, and for a good reason. Teenage girls are the most victimized segment of the American population. According to RAINN, the nation's largest anti-sexual violence organization, Females ages sixteen to nineteen are four times more likely than the general population to be victims of rape, attempted rape, or sexual assault. On top of that, nearly one in four girls (23 percent) who have been in a relationship reported going further sexually than they wanted as a result of pressure. Don't misunderstand me; there are rules for boys who want to date, but girls need to be way more careful based solely on these statistics.

Predatory sexual violence doesn't limit itself to adults. Teens are also perfectly capable of perpetrating violence against one another. Regardless of age, sexual predators often stick to pre-incident indicators that can warn your teen of impending violence. In his bestselling book, *Protecting the Gift, Keeping Children and Teenagers Safe (and Parents Sane)*, author Gavin De Becker states that misplaced trust is a predator's most powerful resource. Your teen's best chance at avoiding sexual violence is to understand and recognize the behaviors that are intended to put them at ease. Here they are:

- **Forced teaming:** This is when the person planning the assault continually uses the word "we" to create a bond that doesn't exist. Phrases such as, "We'll get through this together," "Now we've don't it," or "We make quite the pair, don't we?" are all examples of forced teaming. Teach your teen to be cautious around others who use this tactic and to not be afraid to put a stop to it once it starts. A simple "There's no 'we' yet" should be sufficient.

- **Charm and niceness:** On the surface, there's nothing wrong with this behavior. We always taught our son to be as nice as possible to members of the opposite sex. But to charm is to compel, and trying to compel someone to do something against their will is wrong. Teach your teens to be cautious of anyone who appears to use charm to get what they want.

- **Too many details:** Predators often use this technique when they want to deceive us. When people tell the truth, they don't feel the need to add additional information to support their stories, so pay close attention to what your date is telling you. Too many details about a place they want to take you or a person they want you to meet could signal danger.

- **Typecasting:** Typecasting often involves a minor insult of some sort. "You're probably a good girl who doesn't do anything wrong" is a perfect example. Insinuating that someone should behave in a certain way is a method for manipulating behavior. Predators frequently use this technique to get people to do things they know they shouldn't or wouldn't do otherwise.

- **Loan-sharking:** Loan-sharking refers to offers to help. In and of itself, there's nothing wrong with this. We accept offers of help from people on an almost daily basis. It's when continued offers for help start piling up and the other person starts demanding things in return that this becomes a problem.

- **The unsolicited promise:** Promises are used to convince us of an intention. A guarantee offers some compensation if the other person fails to deliver, but promises offer no such collateral. They offer nothing more than the speaker's desire to convince you of something.

- **Discounting the word "no":** According to Mr. De Becker, this is the most significant signal of all. Ignoring or dismissing the concept of "No" is nothing more than an attempt to gain control.

These pre-incident indicators aren't necessarily indicators of violence but rather of persuasion. The violent or sexual assault comes elsewhere, so a predator's next step after gaining trust would be to get his target in a place where victimization is possible.

When it comes to dating, make sure you talk to your teen about these pre-incident indicators and ensure they understand what these signals mean. Listen closely to intuitive signals you get from the people your teen interacts with. If for some reason you get a bad feeling or start recognizing manipulative behaviors, sit your teen down and have a talk with them about your concerns. It may be the case that your child feels the same way you do about the person they're dating and just needed to hear it from someone else. Trust and communication are key here. Your teen may have to sort through some bad characters to find the person that's right for them. Be there for guidance if they need it, and don't be afraid to have these difficult conversations when the time comes.

Teens in Action

Olivia Jones Causes a Car Accident to Save a Life

Just before Christmas 2018, Olivia Jones pulled up to a red light in Clearwater, Florida. That's when she noticed the driver next to her slumped over. "I thought she was texting because she was looking straight down. And then she started seizing," the Clearwater High School student told local reporters. The woman in the car began shaking violently and foaming at the mouth. Jones noticed the vehicle was starting to slide into the busy intersection, so she came up with a plan and acted immediately. "I opened my door and told people behind me that she was having a seizure, but nobody seemed to care or want to help, so I pulled in front of her and let her hit the back of my car," she said. "She was kind of like seizing out of the car. I took her seat belt off. She had blood and had peed herself. I was on the phone with 9-1-1." Authorities arrived on the scene two minutes after the intentional accident.

Jones was a little worried about what her family would say about the dent when she got home. She says she's typically a good driver. "I haven't gotten in any accidents that were my fault." She now affectionately refers to the dent in her back bumper as her "memory bump." Jones added that she's continually discussing her aspirations of becoming an orthopedic surgeon with her parents. "I always talk to them about who I want to be in the medical field and how I want to save people." Based on her willingness to help others and her quick reactions during this emergency, it looks like Olivia Jones is well on her way.[2]

Practical Exercise

Are You Being Followed?

We've all experienced that "I think this guy's following me" feeling. It's a weird sensation. It's based mostly on intuition, but knowing if you are being followed and verifying that fact is essential for personal safety. During basic training in the Federal Air Marshal Service, we spent a lot of time on what we called "domain awareness training," which culminated in a practical exercise at the local shopping mall. Several civilian role players were given photographs and physical descriptions of us trainees. Then we'd be turned loose to browse around while the role players would follow us from a distance, taking note of everything we did. Our job was to identify the person tailing us without that person knowing they'd been spotted. Then at the end of the exercise, we'd have a lineup and point out the person or people we thought were following us. It was a lot of fun, and the paid role players were very good at their jobs. Just like an actual criminal, they know how to blend in and how to get close without drawing a lot of attention to themselves. Spotting them was a challenge, but we were taught specific techniques to

---

2. Bobby Lewis, "Student Intentionally Causes Car Crash and It May Have Saved a Woman's Life," 10 Tampa Bay, January 17, 2019, https://www.wtsp.com/article/entertainment/places/bobby-lewis-on-the-road/student-intentionally-causes-a-car-crash-and-it-may-have-saved-a-womans-life/67-aeb b4a34-2eea-4fc2-bb69-4254b804c4a2.

draw them out and identify them before they got too close. Now it's time to pass those techniques on to you.

In the Federal Air Marshal Service, we had a simple rule: you never wanted to see the same person in three different places:

First encounter = an accident

Second encounter = a coincidence

Third encounter = you're being followed

Knowing if you're being followed all starts with basic situational awareness. Having your head up and moving like you have a purpose goes a long way in deterring possible attackers, but if you're out and about and feel like someone is following you, you need to verify your suspicions. Here are some specific actions you can take that will flush out and help you to confirm a possible tail:

- **Pace modification:** This one works whether you're walking or driving. If you think you're being followed, gradually start slowing down. Someone who is just going about his or her business will likely pass you by, but someone who is following you will slow down as well to match your pace. If they do, slowly speed back up and see if they stay with you.

- **Surveillance detection routes:** If the person sticks with you after you've modified your speed a couple of times, it's time to mix up your route. If you're walking or driving, make a series of turns that eventually puts you back on your original course. This is known as a boxing maneuver. Only you know that you plan on ending up back in the same spot. If you complete your surveillance detection route and the person you suspect is still behind you, then chances are you're being followed.

- **Window framing:** This one only works when you're walking. If you suspect you're being followed, turn into a store or shop with large windows in the front. Once you're inside, turn and face the windows. If you're being followed, that person will stop to see what you're up to. There you'll be face to face looking at each other through the glass. This usually shocks and surprises the person following you, and their attempts to look casual will turn incredibly awkward. That's a sure-fire way to tell if that person was indeed tailing you.

Regardless of whether or not you're being followed, there are a few things you should be doing when you're out in public to maintain your awareness and deter possible attackers:

- When walking, cross the street from time to time even if you don't need to. Take note of those around you who cross when you do.
- Use natural pauses like crosswalks or red lights to reevaluate your surroundings.
- Occasionally stop at store windows to "browse." Use the reflection to monitor what's behind you without looking overly suspicious.
- Make yourself less predictable by frequently modifying your routes of travel.
- When you park your car, take a few seconds to check your mirrors and determine what's around you before opening the door.

You always want to be aware of your surroundings and mindful of those around you, but at the same time, you don't want to stress yourself out or become overly paranoid. During our training exercises, we knew that we were being followed. It was always eye-opening to stand there looking at the lineup of role players and realize that none of them fit the description of the person you were suspicious of. Sometimes when we suspect we're being followed, everyone starts looking like a bad guy. Remember, situational awareness is critical here. Keep your head up and stay in condition yellow at all times. That's the best way to remain a hard target and spot potential threats before they have a chance to materialize.

Key Points
- Handing over responsibility to your teen should happen in stages. Those transition periods are critical points in a teen's life and an

excellent opportunity for them to gain needed experience under an adult's supervision.

- Before you hand over the keys to the car, sit down with your teen and establish "rules of the road" along with the penalties that come with violating them:
  - No driving or riding with others who are under the influence of drugs or alcohol.
  - No more than two friends in the car at a time (if allowed by the license).
  - No eating or drinking while driving.
  - Keep music at low to moderate volume.
  - Everyone in the vehicle must wear a seat belt at all times.
  - No driving after dark.
  - No driving when tired, angry, or upset.
  - No driving beyond a certain distance from home without getting permission first.
  - No talking on the phone or texting when the vehicle is in motion.
- Review what actions should be taken if your teen encounters an aggressive driver:
  - Never return rude gestures or show anger toward the aggressor.
  - If a person is displaying extreme anger, it is best to remain behind them while in traffic.
  - Be mindful of potential brake checks.
  - Change lanes if the aggressor is tailgating you.
  - If an aggressor motions for you to pull over—don't.
  - Be mindful of traffic and remain aware of your driving at all times—do not break traffic laws to avoid other drivers.
- When it comes to parties, remember the following points:
  - Have a conversation with your teen about situational awareness and intuition before they leave the house. If someone at the party makes your teen feel uncomfortable, remind them that there's a reason for that and that they should always trust their intuition.

○ Let your teen know that they can call you at any time, in any condition, if they or their friends need your help—no questions asked.

○ Make sure they have all of your contact information programmed into their phone. Make sure they also have your number memorized just in case they have to call from another line.

○ Give your contact details to one of your teen's friends.

○ Make sure your child has enough money for an emergency taxi ride home.

• Make your teen aware of pre-incident indicators that accompany coercion and manipulation:

○ Forced teaming

○ Charm and niceness

○ Too many details

○ Typecasting

○ Loan-sharking

○ The unsolicited promise

○ Discounting the word "no"

• These pre-incident indicators aren't necessarily indicators of violence but rather of persuasion. The violent or sexual assault comes elsewhere, so a predator's next step after gaining trust would be to get his target in a place where victimization is possible.

PHASE THREE—Working Together Toward Responsible Independence

"Youth cannot know how age thinks and feels. But old men
are guilty if they forget what it was to be young."
—J. K. ROWLING, *HARRY POTTER
AND THE ORDER OF THE PHOENIX*

7

Responsibility

As TIME MARCHES ON, it becomes more and more difficult for teens to transition into adulthood completely unscathed. The dangers that young people face seem to multiply at an astounding rate. Given the changes in technology, it can be challenging for older generations to keep up. Make no mistake; your child's safety is a group project. We all have a role to play, and both teens and parents need to take their responsibilities seriously.

The great Muppeteer, Jim Henson, once said, "The attitude you have as a parent is what your kids will learn from, more than what you tell them. They don't remember what you try to teach them. They remember what you are." I think that's an important point to make. We parents have an enormous responsibility to our teens. Not only do we have to prepare them for the dangers they could someday face, but we also need to set a positive example when it comes to how they should best protect themselves. We're doing teens a huge disservice if we walk around with our heads buried in our smartphones, ignoring our surroundings. By doing so, we're also ignoring the fact that they are becoming grownups, and they see that. We have to let them know that we're here with them, present in the moment, and ready to help them through that transition to adulthood. Right now, you have a choice to make; you can take the easy road and ignore the changes your child is going through, write it off as a "phase," and institute the "do as I say, not as I do" policy. Or, you can take the hard road and become an active participant in developing your child's defenses. They may not always listen, and be prepared for plenty of eye-rolling when you begin talking about safety and awareness. As I said, this is the hard road, and it's a lot of work, but in the end, I can promise you they'll be thankful for what you've taught them.

In this final phase of the book, we're going to explore parental and teen responsibilities as well as some other factors that impact personal safety. It's crucial at this point that both parents and teens realize the roles they play and how one affects the other. It's easy for parents to expect their teens to act like adults and make the right decisions, but that's not the way it works. When your children make mistakes or do things you disagree with, you shouldn't waste your time wondering, "Why would they do such a thing?" Instead, have them take a look at the consequences of their actions, hold them accountable, and communicate what your expectations will be moving forward. That's the key to establishing boundaries, and as impossible as it may seem, your teen will appreciate the structure and feedback.

Twenty-six-year-old Lauren puts it this way: "Growing up, I was allowed to do anything I wanted to do. There were hardly any rules. When it came to school, my mom let me decide if I felt like going to school or not. I literally got straight F's," says Lauren. "I resent my mom because she never taught me any life skills. I didn't even know how to write a check . . . I have so much resentment toward my mom that our relationship is falling apart. I do try to be civil toward my mom, but underneath it all, I really only feel anger."[1]

Imagine being a teen with no rules or limits. What would your life be like had you not had some structure in your adolescent years? I

---

1. "A Powerful Reminder of Why Teens Need Rules and Limits," *Dr. Phil*, nd, https://www.drphil.com/show-pages/why_teens_need_rules/.

know for a fact that I probably wouldn't be sitting here writing this book. When it comes to parental responsibilities, there are four things all parents should be doing:

- **Act like a parent:** Remember, you are in charge. There's nothing more rewarding than watching your teen thrive and grow, but if your teen doesn't know where the line is between parent and pal, they're much more likely to push boundaries. Eventually, they'll push too far and end up putting themselves in dangerous situations. At that point, reasserting your parental authority becomes almost impossible. It doesn't matter if your child is two or twenty; being consistent as a parent is a significant responsibility, so take it seriously.
- **Set the rules:** As I mentioned earlier, whether they know it or not, your teen will appreciate structure. They may not voice that appreciation until they're older, but I promise you, it's there. The house rules are something parents should firmly establish well before their child hits their teen years. Rules about how far they're allowed to stray from the house, restricted areas, curfews, and the consequences of negative action should all be in place very early on. As long as your child knows why they're in place (their safety), it will be easier for them to understand those rules when they're older.
- **Enforce the rules:** This one is an absolute must! Have you ever watched a parent tell their toddler, "Don't make me count to three . . . one . . . two . . . I'm at two, you'd better calm down . . . two and a half . . . I'm serious. I'm almost at three. Don't test me!" The behavior they're trying to correct only continues, and the parent is left confused and frustrated as to why their child won't listen. The answer is obvious: it's because they refuse to enforce the rules, and the child knows it. If a failure to follow through on consequences continues, parents can expect more bad behavior as the child gets older. We've already covered the fact that as teens start testing the limits of what they can and cannot do, they sometimes put themselves in dangerous situations. Parents are fully responsible for their children's safety,

even if that child looks like an adult. Ensure your teen knows the rules, why they're in place, and what happens when those rules are broken. Be firm in that.

- **Be willing to negotiate:** It's okay to be flexible. If your teen is following the rules and demonstrating a reasonable level of maturity and responsibility, it's okay to back off from time to time. If they come to you with a request to break curfew and stay out later with friends, be willing to have that conversation. Show them that you appreciate their good behavior and you're willing to reward that. But keep in mind that this is something that has to be requested and approved upfront, not something that's discussed or justified after the fact. Remember, safety always comes first. You need to know where your teen is and when.

The process of helping children take responsibility and make decisions is crucial for parents. Still, parents aren't the only ones with responsibilities. Teens also have obligations when it comes to maintaining their safety as well as their parent's trust. Have open discussions about personal safety and the things they feel they can handle. Once the boundaries have been set and the rules established, make sure they understand what their specific roles are. How quickly you begin to hand over responsibility to your teen will depend on things like your own comfort level, your family norms, and your child's level of maturity. Ideally, you and your teen should both feel comfortable with the shift in responsibility and the pace at which it takes place.

According to raisingchildren.net, you might need to experiment to work out when and in what areas your teen is ready for more responsibility. An excellent way to start is to use family meetings to give your teen a real voice in important decisions. This helps your child feel valued. It's also a good way for you to learn more about how they deal with choices. When assigning responsibilities, here are some other things to consider.

- Your teen's level of maturity
- Their ability to learn from experience
- The level of risk they're exposed to
- The impact their actions may have on others
- Your family values

When you begin assigning responsibility to your teen, be careful to maintain a balance between too much and too little. Too little responsibility, and they have no chance to make decisions and learn through experience. Too much, too fast, and teenagers might end up making bad decisions and undermining their confidence by doing things they're not ready for. If you and your teenager aren't quite sure about a new responsibility, discuss it, but assert that the final decision belongs to the parent.

So far, we've covered the basics of situational awareness and some of the things you need to consider as you maneuver through the transition of responsibilities. Before we drill down into the topics of communication and teamwork, let's take a closer look at what happens when teens don't take their responsibilities seriously. Your child needs to understand up front that once they gain responsibility, they also bear the weight of their actions. This is known as accountability.

Teens in Action

Thirteen-Year-Old Kaleb Saves His Friend from
Drowning at a Pool Party

One sunny afternoon in Hall County, Georgia, thirteen-year-old best friends Kaleb Reeves and Nick Williams attended a poolside birthday party. As with most pool parties, the kids got a little playful, and someone decided to push Nick into the deep end of the pool. Unfortunately, Nick couldn't swim. Kaleb told local reporters that when his friends didn't see Williams resurface, they started to panic. That's when Reeves took action.

"We were just having fun jumping in the water, and some of my friends on the balcony were saying that Nick was under the water, drowning," Reeves said. "I was confused because I've never seen him get in the water."

Reeves said Williams's sister was able to feel him with her foot.

"I dove in and grabbed him, and I pulled him up," Reeves said. "I got up under him and pushed him out of the water."

One of the mothers at the party saw what was happening and helped pull Nick from the pool. Then she started administering CPR. Williams was rushed to the local hospital, where he made a full recovery.

"I mean, I wasn't really scared because I knew I was doing the right thing, and I had to get him out of the water . . . I love him, and I'm glad he's okay," Kaleb said.

Kaleb's mother, April Reeves, later told reporters, "I'm just very proud of him and, you know, I just see that the Lord put Kaleb in the right place, at the right time, and it's a blessing that everything turned out alright and that Nick is here with us."

Williams's family later called Reeves their "guardian angel."[2]

---

2. "Thirteen-Year-Old Hero Saves Best Friend from Drowning at Pool Party," WFTv 9 ABC, nd, https://www.wftv.com/news/trending-now/13yearold -hero-saves-best-friend-from-drowning-at-pool-party/952482607/.

Practical Exercise

The Four Corners Game

In my second book, *Spotting Danger Before It Spots Your Kids*, I recommended implementing a family game night. Games spark your child's imagination and serve as a vehicle for education. They can help to improve memory, spatial awareness, comprehension, analytical thinking, problem-solving, and decision-making in a way that both the parent and the child can appreciate. More importantly, game night helps to reconnect the family. Now that your children are older, game night might not be as cool as it used to be, but at this point, your teen should realize what these games are for and what they help to accomplish.

When it comes to our senses, sight plays the larger role in situational awareness, but the more we get our other senses involved, the better off we'll be in terms of personal safety. The four corners game is an excellent way to develop your teen's spatial awareness using nothing more than their hearing and intuition. Here's how it's played.

This game works best when it's played with five or more people. Use any four-cornered room in your house, and pick one person to be "it." Place that person in the center of the room with a blindfold in their hand. Everyone else can stand in the corner of their choosing. Let the person in the center get a good look at where everyone is. Once they're ready, they place the blindfold over their eyes and count out loud to twenty. As they count, everyone else in the room moves around to different corners. Do this as quietly as possible, but make it a point to pass as near to the person in the center as possible without touching them. There are a lot of options here. You can choose to stay where you are, move to a different side of the room, or group up in one corner with others. Hearing plays a major role in this game, but their intuition will begin to play a larger role in knowing when people are moving around them in the absence of sight.

Once the person in the center reaches twenty, everyone has to stop where they are. The "it" person then has to point to the corner where they believe the most people are. The goal is to pinpoint each person's locations in the room and name precisely who's standing where. The more you play, the better you get at it. Make it fun, and play a quick game or two before your kid sets out for their next get-together with friends. It's unrealistic to believe that your teenager can keep an eye on everyone around them all the time, but by developing their other senses to help keep track of people, you're improving their spatial and situational awareness in general. This, in turn, keeps them safer and can allow you to rest a little easier when they start going out on their own.

Key Points
- Parental responsibilities include the following:
  - Act like a parent: Remember that you are in charge.
  - Set the rules: Whether they know it or not, your teen will appreciate structure. The house rules are something that parents should firmly establish well before their child hits their teen years.
  - Enforce the rules: Parents are fully responsible for the safety of their children, even if that child looks like an adult. Make sure your teen knows the rules, why they're in place, and what happens when those rules are broken.
  - Be willing to negotiate: It's okay to be flexible. If your teen is following the rules and demonstrating a reasonable level of maturity and responsibility, it's okay to back off from time to time. Show them that you appreciate their good behavior and that you're willing to reward that.
- When assigning responsibilities, here are some other things to consider.
  - Your teen's level of maturity
  - Their ability to learn from experience
  - The legality of their actions
  - The level of risk they're exposed to
  - The impact their actions may have on others
  - Your family values
- When you begin to assign responsibility to your teen, be careful to maintain a balance between too much and too little.

8

Accountability

RESPONSIBILITY AND ACCOUNTABILITY differ in one significant way. Responsibility means dedicating yourself to the completion of a specific task. That task can be either long or short term. For example, long-term responsibilities would be to raise healthy, productive children. Examples of short-term responsibilities could be getting to work on time, finishing homework, or reading this book. Accountability, on the other hand, is taking ownership of the results of that duty. Perhaps you never take the responsibility of getting to work on time seriously. Suppose down the road you're passed up for a promotion, or even worse, fired. In that case, that's a consequence of your lack of responsibility, and you are the sole person accountable for that. When parents teach their teens to be responsible and hold them accountable for their actions, they're helping them develop into caring, conscientious adults. Without these traits, both teens and adults become complacent and dependent. They tend to blame others for the outcomes they experience and look for ways to avoid their obligations. Not only obligations to their family, their school, or their job, but to themselves, and that can be a very dangerous quality when it comes to personal safety.

No one grows in their personal lives without accountability. Teenagers who are just starting to realize some of the negative consequences of their actions may tend to blame others, refuse to follow rules they find unfair, or find ways to justify their behavior regardless of its impact on others. All of this can add to tension and discomfort at home and severely strain the parent/teen relationship. In the following chapter, we will cover the importance of communication, but before we can have useful discussions about situational awareness and personal safety, both teens and parents must be willing and able to recognize their flaws. As an adult, it's crucial to your teen's development that you find ways to instill accountability. A very enlightening article from middleearthnj.org recommends these eight steps when it comes to instilling accountability in your teen:

- **Demonstrate personal responsibility:** Role modeling is the most effective tool parents have for teaching their teens anything. Any value you want your teen to have, demonstrate it in your everyday life. So if you want your teen to take responsibility for their actions, you should do the same. Avoid blaming others. Follow the rules, and don't avoid the consequences if you break them. If you make a mistake, admit it, apologize, and make amends if possible. For example, if you accidentally bang the car door next to you in the parking lot, leave a note.
- **Create a culture of accountability in your family:** Your family has its own culture that reflects your values, expectations, rules, and hopes. If you want an accountable teen, then each member of your family must be responsible for their actions and behaviors, each family member must be responsible for following rules and expectations, and each must be responsible for how they respond to stressful or frustrating situations. No one in the family should be allowed to change the rules to fit their own needs or feelings.
- **Establish boundaries:** You must provide your children clear and firm rules and expectations so they are aware of the consequences

of their actions. Your teen must know that if they choose to break the rules, there will be a consequence for that choice. Of course, this only works if you don't give in or give up just because your teen whines or promises to behave. You must see the consequence through in order to see the behavior change.

- **Be involved in their life:** Research consistently shows that teens with involved parents are more likely to be responsible and do better in school and less likely to engage in risky behaviors, such as drugs, crime, and sex. Establish open, friendly, and honest communication with your children from a young age. Learn about their interests and attend their activities. Showing that you care about and support your teen helps them feel valued, and this in turn makes them more eager to engage with you and want to please you.

- **Don't be overinvolved:** There is a fine line between showing your teen you support them and micromanaging their lives. As parents, many of us do things for our kids today that we were able and expected to do for ourselves when we were children. Our parents didn't feel the need to negotiate with our sports coach, solve our every problem, or entertain us in our free time. We should let our teens manage their own lives.

- **Refrain from rescuing your teen:** It is so painful for us, as parents, to watch our children go through difficult circumstances, and we typically want to jump in and fix things. While this is a natural reaction to protecting someone we love, it's one of the worst things you can do as a parent. When your child is a teenager, your role becomes more of a coach. You want to guide and support your teen through their difficulty while still allowing them to discover their capabilities. If we step in, we stop the learning process and deprive our teens of developing the courage needed to try new things and solve problems. Your teen needs to learn now—before leaving your home as a young adult—how to manage obstacles in life. They need to have experience overcoming a difficulty on their own to gain confidence in themselves and realize they are capable. When you rescue your teen, you are inadvertently communicating that you don't think they can handle challenges, and your teen will begin to doubt their own abilities. Your teen will learn to expect that others will take care of things for them, and they will become a master of avoiding challenges instead of facing them.

- **Allow natural consequences:** No matter how painful, you must let your teen be responsible for the good and bad decisions they have made. It might feel cruel, but it's the very best parenting you can offer. If a teen gets a ticket for speeding, he should pay the fine, not you. If he doesn't have the money, he will need to find a way to earn it or lose his license. If your teen procrastinates on a big project, do not do the task for them. If your teen didn't prepare for an exam, don't make excuses to the teacher and beg for a second chance. Let them receive the lousy grade and handle the results. This way, kids will learn how to take responsibility for their actions and deal with the consequences.
- **Praise them when they demonstrate responsibility:** Positive reinforcement of your teen's actions to show responsibility will encourage them to continue the behavior. Never underestimate the power of a compliment.[1]

All of these tips are fantastic ways to instill accountability, but don't let this slip into a one-sided issue. Parents have to be held accountable as well. If your teen stays out too late or breaks one of the house rules, take a look at the events leading up to that action. Was there effective communication between you and your teen regarding your expectations? Did you adequately emphasize the repercussions your teen would face by neglecting the rules? Did your teen understand the left and right limits you had set earlier? If you're unsure about any of these questions, own up

---

1. "Eight Ways to Instill Accountability in Teens," Middle Earth, September 25, 2017, https://middleearthnj.org/2017/09/25/8-ways-to-instill-accountability -in-teens/.

to the fact that you may be partly responsible for the lack of communication. Your teen's safety is dependent on you setting a positive example and clearly articulating what's expected of them. That brings us to the next point about developing responsible independence: communication.

Teens in Action
Sixteen-Year-Old Girl Fights Off Attacker

One evening in Kent County, Washington, a sixteen-year-old girl was walking home. She turned a corner and noticed a man standing by a dark SUV parked along her path. It was almost midnight, and something about the situation felt off. The SUV's motor was running, and the man was watching the girl intently. Her intuition immediately told her she was in danger, so she turned to run away. That's when the man grabbed her by the throat and forced her into the vehicle. He started trying to remove her pants and told her not to scream. The girl didn't listen. She began kicking and screaming as loudly as she could. She was able to force the man off her and started honking the horn to get someone's attention. Eventually, she was able to escape the SUV, but the man continued to pursue her. He grabbed by her shirt, but the girl turned and violently scratched the man's face. That allowed her to slip out of her shirt and escape his grip. Knowing he couldn't control the teen, the man fled back to his vehicle and made an escape. The young girl was able to flag down a car for help and had them call 911. She was able to give a full description of both the man and the SUV. She told police that the man was about 6-feet-2-inches tall, with salt and pepper shoulder-length hair. She thought he was between fifty and fifty-five years old and was driving an older, dark-colored four-door SUV similar to a Toyota 4-Runner. That gave the police enough information to track the man down and eventually make an arrest.[2]

---

2. "Man Who Attempted to Rape and Kidnap Sixteen-Year-Old Girl Arrested," KOMO News, October 4, 2018, https://komonews.com/news/local /man-who-attempted-to-rape-and-kidnap-16-year-old-kent-girl-arrested-poli ce-say.

All children are different, but it's important to prepare them to fight if the situation calls for it. My kids always enjoyed these little fight sessions. We had a large lifelike punching bag set up in the garage. I'd work with them on the proper way to throw a palm heal strike to the nose and how to deliver a kick to the groin. I'd let them scream at the top of their lungs while they attacked the bag. I encouraged them to be as aggressive as they wanted; nothing was off-limits. They always had a blast doing this type of thing, but I always made sure they understood the context. These types of actions are a last resort, and they're to be used only when you feel you are in danger. Just like the girl in this story, you have to understand that sometimes things can catch you off guard. You have to prepare your children to defend themselves violently should the need arise. It may not be something you're comfortable with, but it could possibly save their lives.

Practical Exercise

Eyewitness Test

The next time you're out running an errand with your teen or wandering around the local mall, take note of a store employee. Pay close attention to his or her physical description as well as their manner of dress, name tag, and location. Once you have as many details as possible, casually point that person out. A simple "take a look at that guy" will suffice. Then continue about your way. Wait a half-hour or so and then quiz your teen on what they can remember about that person. Have them be as descriptive as possible.

- How tall were they?
- What color was their hair?
- How much did they weigh?
- How old did they look?
- Describe what they were wearing.
- Did they have any distinctive features?

- Did you happen to notice if they were wearing a name tag?
- What was their name?

This exercise will help your teen pay closer attention to the people they interact with. That's a handy skill to have should they ever be called upon to act as an eyewitness to a violent or criminal event. Just like the girl in this chapter's "Teens in Action" story, being able to remember the physical characteristics of an attacker, even when under tremendous stress, may not stop what's happening, but it can certainly help apprehend the assailant before they can commit another crime against someone else.

Key Points
Eight steps to instilling accountability in your teen:

1. Demonstrate personal responsibility: Role modeling is the most effective tool parents have for teaching their teens anything. Any value you want your teen to have, demonstrate it in your everyday life.

2. Create a culture of accountability in your family: If you want an accountable teen, then each member of your family must be responsible for their actions and behaviors, each family member must be responsible for following rules and expectations, and each must be responsible for how they respond to stressful or frustrating situations.

3. Establish boundaries: You must provide your children clear and firm rules and expectations so they are aware of the consequences of their actions. Your teen must know that if they choose to break the rules, there will be a consequence for that choice.

4. Be involved in their life: Learn about their interests and attend their activities. Showing that you care about and support your teen helps them feel valued, and this, in turn, makes them more eager to engage with you and want to please you.

5. But don't be overinvolved: There is a fine line between showing your teen that you support them and micromanaging their lives. As parents, many of us do things for our kids today that we were able and expected to do for ourselves when we were children.

6. Refrain from rescuing your teen: When your child is a teenager, your role becomes more of a coach. You want to guide and support your teen through their difficulty while still allowing them to discover their own capabilities. If we step in, we stop the learning process and deprive our teens of the chance to develop the courage they'll need to try new things and solve problems.

7. Allow natural consequences: No matter how painful, you must let your teen be responsible for the good and bad decisions they make. It might feel cruel, but it's the very best parenting you can offer.

8. Praise them when they demonstrate responsibility: Positive reinforcement of your teen's actions to show responsibility will encourage them to continue the behavior. Never underestimate the power of a compliment

9

Communication

ATTEMPTING TO MAINTAIN A HEALTHY and open relationship with your teen is one of the most important things you can do as a parent. I say "attempting" because the teenage years can be challenging, to say the least. Much like a toddler, teens are doing new and exciting things; they're finding new ways to express themselves, and they don't take the word "no" very lightly. As your teen transitions into adulthood, staying close as a family becomes more difficult. Somewhere between teens wanting to break away and parents trying to hold everything together lies fertile ground for growing a stronger relationship. That bond not only strengthens your relationship, it also fosters confidence, which is something they'll need when it comes to protecting themselves from danger. Finding that mutually agreeable middle ground all begins with communication.

9.1 Parental Communication

It's easy for us parents to give in to the hardships of day-to-day life and close ourselves off. You may not see it happening, but I can guarantee your teen does, and it's only in hindsight that we see how our words and actions affect our children. I know that I've personally let my emotions get the best of me and resorted to harsh words and short answers when open and honest discussion would have been more appropriate. These types of reactions to issues create a very uncomfortable divide between parents and children. I clearly remember coming to the realization that I could possibly be the reason my teens didn't want to open up in front of me. It was a hard pill to swallow, but it forced me to become more self-aware and take more time to talk openly with my kids about the things that were bothering them. Some of the problems they wanted to talk about were uncomfortable for me to hear and ran much deeper than I could have imagined. It can be tough to talk to your children about their problems, but believe me when I tell you, that their mental and physical well-being depends on having someone they trust to open up to. It takes a lot of work, but there are ways for parents to become better communicators. Rachel Ehmke of The Child Mind Institute recommends the following when talking with your teen about the issues that are bothering them:

- **Listen.** If you are curious about what's going on in your teen's life, asking direct questions might not be as useful as simply sitting back and listening. Kids are more likely to be open with their parents if they don't feel pressured to share information. Remember, even an offhand comment about something that happened during the day is their way of reaching out, and you're likely to hear more if you stay open and interested.
- **Validate their feelings.** It is often our tendency to try to solve problems for our kids or downplay their disappointments. But saying something like, "She wasn't right for you anyway" after a romantic disappointment can feel dismissive. Instead, show kids that you understand and empathize by reflecting the comment back: "Wow, that does sound difficult."

- **Show trust.** Teens want to be taken seriously, especially by their parents. Look for ways to show that you trust your teen. Asking them for a favor shows that you rely on them. Volunteering a privilege shows you think they can handle it. Letting your kid know you have faith in them will boost their confidence and make them more likely to rise to the occasion.
- **Don't be a dictator.** You still get to set the rules, but be ready to explain them. While pushing the boundaries is natural for teenagers, hearing your thoughtful explanation about why parties on school nights aren't allowed will make the rule seem more reasonable.
- **Give praise.** Parents tend to praise children more when they are younger, but adolescents need the self-esteem boost just as much. Teenagers might act like they're too cool to care about what their parents think, but the truth is they still want your approval. Also, looking for positive and encouraging opportunities is good for the relationship, especially when it is feeling strained.
- **Control your emotions.** It's easy for tempers to flare when your teen is being rude, but you should never respond in kind. Remember that you're the adult, and teens are less able to control their emotions or think clearly when they're upset. Count to ten or take some deep breaths before responding. If you're both too upset to talk, hit pause until you've had a chance to calm down.
- **Do things together.** Talking isn't the only way to communicate. It's great during these adolescent years if you can spend time doing something you both enjoy, whether it's cooking or hiking or going to the movies, without talking about anything personal. Kids need to know that they can be in proximity to you and share positive experiences without having to worry about intrusive questions or if you'll call them out for something.
- **Share regular meals.** Sitting down to eat a meal together as a family is another excellent way to stay close. Dinner conversations

give every family member a chance to check-in and talk casually about sports, television, or school. Kids who feel comfortable talking to parents about everyday things are more likely to open up when discussing more challenging topics.

- **Be observant.** It's normal for kids to go through some changes as they mature, but pay attention if you notice changes to their mood, behavior, energy level, or appetite. Likewise, take note if they stop wanting to do things that used to make them happy or if you notice them isolating themselves. If you see a change in your teen's daily ability to function, ask about it and be supportive (without being judgmental). They may need your help, and it could be a sign that they need to talk to a mental health professional.[1]

These are all great ways to strengthen relationships and create a communication pattern with your child, but no one likes a one-sided conversation. As young adults, teens also have to be willing to open up and not shut themselves off to the information their parents are trying to convey.

9.2 Teen Communication

This section is specifically for teens. As most of you know, talking and listening don't go smoothly every time. Some parents are easy to talk to, some are great listeners, and some are harder to approach. But some of what happens during a conversation depends on you. Since communication is a two-way street, the way you talk can influence how well a parent listens and understands you. The best way to gain your parent's attention and have them vested in the issues you're facing is by approaching them in a way that demonstrates your level of maturity. This is especially effective when it comes to discussing difficult topics. Here are some guidelines recommended by Dr. D'Arcy Lyness of kidshealth.org that can help you to better communicate with your parents:

---

1. Rachel Emke, "Tips for Communicating with Your Teen," Child Mind Institute, nd, https://childmind.org/article/tips-communicating-with-teen/.

- **Be clear and direct.** Be as clear as you can about what you think, feel, and want. Give details that can help parents understand your situation. They can listen better or be more helpful if they get what you mean and what's really going on.

- **Be honest.** If you're always honest, a parent will be likely to believe what you say. If you sometimes hide the truth or add too much drama, parents will have a harder time believing what you tell them. If you lie, they'll find it hard to trust you.

- **Try to understand their point of view.** If you have a disagreement, can you see your parents' side? If you can, say so. Telling parents you understand their views and feelings helps them be willing to see yours as well.

- **Try not to argue or whine.** Using a friendly and respectful tone makes it more likely parents will listen and take what you say seriously. It also makes it more likely that they'll talk to you in the same way. Of course, this is hard for any of us (adults included) when we're feeling heated about something. If you think your emotions might get the better of you, do something to blow off steam before talking: Go for a run. Cry. Hit your pillow. Do whatever it takes to sound calm when you need to.[2]

This is all great advice, but I've discovered over the years that the biggest hurdle to effective communication is close-mindedness. We all view things from our own perspective. If we expect to reach some common ground and be helpful to one another, we have to take the time to look at problems from the other person's point of view. When we're talking about topics that affect your teen's safety and security, it's easy for adults to just shut things down to be on the safe side. That's no way to let your child grow. Remember, we're here to help with that transition into adulthood, not stop it in its tracks. We all have to be on the same

---

2. D'Arcy Lyness, "Talking to Your Parents or Other Adults," Nemour's Children's Health, nd, https://kidshealth.org/en/teens/talk-to-parents.html.

page when it comes to responsibility and personal safety. That brings us to our next topic, teamwork.

Teens in Action
High School Freshman Called Hero for Saving Bus Driver and Classmates

For fourteen-year-old Matt Stauffer, Tuesday started off just like any other school day. He got on his school bus around 7:30 am, but as he was walking to his seat, he noticed students on the bus looked scared and seemed panicked.

"So I turned around, and the bus driver was like leaning out of his seat, and only his seat belt was holding him up," Stauffer said.

Stauffer said he ran to help the driver then realized the man's foot was stuck on the gas pedal.

"I reached up, turned the bus off, and then I put the keys in my pocket. No one else could get them," Stauffer said.

Still holding the driver, Stauffer told the other students to get off the bus and call 911.

"Once they saw I was taking control, they all listened to me, and they got off the bus, and they all stayed in one area," Stauffer said.

Paramedics soon arrived on the scene and rushed the bus driver to the hospital to be treated for an unknown medical condition. Superintendent Dr. Brian Gasper said students are routinely given bus evacuation drills, so they know what to do in case of an emergency. They just had one of those drills last week.

"It's refreshing to know that the students paid attention and employed the skills that we gave them last week, but also just snapping into action and the focus that he and the other students exhibited," Dr. Gasper said.

"I wasn't really thinking. I was just acting, just doing what I thought was right," Stauffer said.

This story highlights the importance of practice; much like the "what if" games we mentioned earlier, rehearsing for bad situations can decrease reaction times and speed up reactions. Young Matt Stauffer was faced with a problem that he probably wasn't expecting, but lives were saved that day through his action and leadership.[3]

Practical Exercise

The Self-Assessment for Teens

Earlier, we covered the importance of knowing how predatory criminals think and what they look for in their victims. It's crucial that teens routinely evaluate themselves and adjust their level of awareness based on the following factors:

- WHO: Are you routinely exposed to the people you identified as someone who may want to hurt you? If so, try to minimize that contact as much as possible.
- WHAT: When you find yourself in the vicinity of these people, are you in possession of something they may find valuable? Always try to minimize observable value when out in public.
- WHEN: Are there specific times you feel you may be vulnerable to attack? If so, be sure to eliminate all distractions and focus on your surroundings.
- WHERE: Are there places or positions you've put yourself into that could possibly make you more vulnerable to attack? Once these areas of your life are identified, make it a point to avoid them if at all possible. If avoidance isn't an option, be sure to raise your awareness level and focus on what's happening around you when you're in these areas.

Using these points, continually identify the people, places, and circumstances that could pose a risk to your safety. When you find yourself exposed to one of these risks, make an effort to modify your body

---

3. "High School Freshman Called Hero for Saving Bus Driver, Classmates," ABC 11 Eyewitness News, March 15, 2019, https://abc11.com/student-hero-teen-saves-bus-driver-rescued/5195726/.

language and behavioral patterns to present a hard target to any potential attackers.

Key Points
- Remember the following when talking with your teen about the issues that are bothering them:
  - Listen.
  - Validate their feelings.
  - Show trust.
  - Don't be a dictator.
  - Give praise.
  - Control your emotions.
  - Do things together.
  - Share regular meals.
  - Be observant.
- When communicating with parents, teens should remember the following:
  - Be clear and direct.
  - Be honest.
  - Try to understand their point of view.
  - Try not to argue or whine.

10

Teamwork

As a federal air marshal, I never sat on the plane alone; I had a team. We frequently traveled at five hundred miles per hour, 30,000 feet in the air, with no backup, but we had each other's back. We had trained together for every conceivable scenario, we knew how to communicate effectively while in flight, and we were keenly aware of each other's strengths and weaknesses. That level of teamwork made us much more efficient when it came to detecting and defeating dangerous situations. Along those same lines, family members who work together can also balance each other's strengths and weaknesses, which will bring everyone closer together as a team. We all have a role to play when it comes to teen safety. Being secure in our environment is a challenging task, but it's much easier if you know you have a strong support system backing you up.

When it comes to building teamwork within your family, keep in mind that everyone has different skills and talents. Each family member has something unique they bring to the table. The key to assigning responsibilities and strengthening communication hinges on what those talents are and how they can help everyone else. Let's say, for instance, that Dad is really good with cars. He can be assigned the responsibility of ensuring everyone's vehicle is in good working order and that the older kids know how to perform basic maintenance. Mom may be really good with money. She can teach the kids how to budget, prioritize purchases, and manage a checking account. The oldest child may be skilled at math and can help the younger children with homework. You get the picture. We all have strengths and weaknesses, but everyone comes out stronger by working together and combining efforts.

Safety and security function the same way. As you work with your kids to develop their situational awareness, note their strengths and weaknesses. Work diligently to correct those weaknesses that pose a threat to their well-being, like an inability to stop looking at their phone or difficulty focusing on the task at hand. Take a moment to communicate why these behaviors pose a threat and how they can be corrected. Remember, you're the parent, and you're the one who decides how much control is given to your teen and when. Make sure you're working with them to hone their awareness skills and keeping them concentrated on the things that can affect their safety. As you're doing so, keep reinforcing the benefits of teamwork. Ann Benjamin, a licensed professional counselor, points out that when developing teamwork among family members, parents need to emphasize the following:

- **Shared vision.** What is required of the members of this family and why?
- **Trust among members.** Admit mistakes and keep promises to improve team strength.
- **Establish expectations and guidelines.** Clearly state the responsibilities of each family member.
- **Communication skills and conflict resolution.** Set up guidelines for communication and allow all members to express thoughts and opinions; practice active listening skills.
- **Personal leadership.** Parents need to be aware that each team member is an individual and may require a different engagement style. Individuals need to be responsible for their own areas.
- **Appreciation of differences.** Listen to the family team members when they suggest alternative or new ways of accomplishing goals. Value each team member for their strengths and skills.
- **Accountability and consequences.** Clearly define each team member's expected and resulting consequences if and when goals are not met.
- **Mentoring others.** Each member of your family team has something valuable to teach the other team members.

There is indeed strength in numbers, and nowhere is this truer than within the family unit. The catch is, when it comes to family, you can't pick your teams. We get what we get, and we all have an obligation to keep that team strong and working in the same direction. We owe it to each other to have one another's back and keep an eye on what's going on in each other's lives.

Situational awareness is a responsibility that extends well beyond the walls of our homes, but home is where it all starts. You have an obligation to your teens to help them get through this transition into adulthood. Keep an eye on them and pay attention to those baseline behaviors within your family. When something seems wrong or out of place, listen to your intuition. Call a team meeting and make sure everyone is okay. Remember the tips we covered on responsibility, accountability, and communication. Every team needs a leader. Be the leader that your teens look up to and respect. As your team strengthens, you'll notice your children taking on those same leadership qualities. With that comes the level of competence and confidence they'll need as they move forward.

Teens in Action

Grace Henerey Saves Her Friend

The quick-thinking actions of a sixteen-year-old girl may have saved her friend's life. When Grace Henerey's twelve-year-old neighbor Grayson fell off her bike and started having a seizure, Grace didn't have to think about what she was going to do; instinct took over, and Grace sprang into action.

"She wasn't breathing, and she wasn't blinking, and her lips started to turn blue," Grace said. She never had any formal CPR training, but her mom taught her what to do years ago when she wanted to start babysitting.

"She just sprung into action. Took off her shirt, put it under her head, put pressure on the wound," Grace's mother said. Grace gave Grayson mouth-to-mouth resuscitation while her mom called 911. Grace's mom later stated, "At the time, we were really concentrated on seeing what was happening and taking care of Grayson, but after that, I was proud, thankful, tearful. So many emotions at one time, it was just overwhelming."

Grayson had to be life-flighted to the hospital where she remained for four days. She got fifteen stitches in her head, and doctors are still trying to figure out precisely what happened. But Grayson says it was her friend who saved her life.

"If she wasn't there, there was no telling what would have happened," said Grayson.

Grace is just glad her friend is okay.

"She's like a little sister to me, and I love her with all my heart," said Grace.

Grayson says she's feeling fine now; she was out riding bikes with Grace a few weeks later.[1]

Practical Exercise

Route Planning

Knowing your way to and from the locations you frequent is a fundamental skill. Make it a point to find as many different routes as possible and vary your travel patterns. This makes you less predictable and works whether you're walking, driving, or using public transportation. Here are a few things you can do when you're on foot to help raise your awareness level, decrease reactionary times, and improve your defensive posture.

- Keep your head up and continuously scan your environment for baseline anomalies.
- Don't approach corners too closely. Give yourself as much space as possible to help with visibility and give yourself more time to react should you encounter something unexpected.
- Avoid unnecessary distractions. If you must be on your phone, put yourself in a position where no one can approach you unexpectedly.
- Keep an eye on people's hands. Hands are what can hurt you.
- Pay close attention to the way you walk. Remember to stand up straight and move with purpose. Looking sure of yourself makes you look more like a hard target, which is a great way to deter potential attackers.

During your daily activities, frequently reevaluate your posture and walking patterns. As this becomes more natural, you can then add mental tasks such as counting exits and identifying potential escape routes to sharpen your senses and improve your overall awareness.

---

1. Kaitlyn Ross, "Teen Saves Friend's Life with Quick Thinking," 11 Alive, May 15, 2014, https://www.11alive.com/article/news/local/teen-saves-friends -life-with-quick-thinking/85-253129795.

Key Points

- When it comes to building teamwork within your family, keep in mind that everyone has different skills and talents. Each family member has something unique they bring to the table.
- When developing teamwork among family members, parents need to emphasize the following things:
  - Shared vision
  - Trust among members
  - Established expectations and guidelines
  - Communication skill and conflict resolution
  - Personal leadership
  - Appreciation of differences
  - Accountability and consequences
  - Mentoring others
- Keep an eye on your teens and pay attention to those baseline behaviors within your family. When something seems wrong or out of place, listen to your intuition.

Conclusion

"Train up a child in the way he should go: and when he is old,
he will not depart from it."
PROVERBS 22:6 (NKJV)

For close to two decades, I worked as a federal air marshal. My job was to keep Americans safe as they flew to and from their destinations. I would blend into my environment and watch intently for any indicators that something bad was about to happen. When I wasn't in the air, I trained diligently, keeping myself ready to fight should the need ever arise. Back then, situational awareness was front and center in my life, and it served me well. Now that I'm retired, I still train, and I still practice those techniques that kept me and my teammates secure for so many years. I do this not because I have a hard time letting go of the past, but because I know that I have kids of my own, as well as nephews, nieces, and cousins who could possibly face threats of their own one of these days. I want nothing more than for them to be confident and prepared. I want to set an example for them and teach them that they don't have to walk around afraid. I want that same thing for you.

The world can be a crazy place, and there are plenty of dangerous people out there just looking for someone to take advantage of. They prey on the weak, the timid, and the unaware. My greatest hope is that I can pass some of what I've learned about situational awareness and safety on to you and that you, in turn, can pass that information on to your children. Parents face a lot of hardship when it comes to raising teenagers, but there's also a lot of rewards. Nothing fills a parent's heart more with pride than seeing their teen transform into a strong, independent, responsible adult, watching them make good decisions, or merely being accountable for their bad ones. It's a process, and it's not always easy, but it can be done.

Your teen's security starts with the examples that you set for them. You have to be situationally aware yourself if you ever expect your children to learn what it means to be secure in their environment. I encourage you to study the concepts that I've outlined in this book and to have open and honest discussions with your kids about the issues they may be facing. Teenagers deal with a lot of adversity, and it's critical that we adults stay in touch with what's happening right now as opposed to just rehashing how "things used to be."

From fourteen to forty, we all have our struggles. Work together with your teen and let them know that they don't have to go it alone. Show them that you're capable of being there for them when things get tough. Help them to find their own way through life and keep them aware of what's happening around them. I promise you that the day will come when you have to watch your teen walk out that front door alone, but you can do so with confidence knowing that you've given them the tools they need to be safe, situationally aware, and responsibly independent. When that day finally arrives, don't panic, take a deep breath, relax, and enjoy some peace and quiet. We both know you've earned it.

Acknowledgments

I BEGIN THIS THIRD BOOK in the "Heads Up" situational awareness series four months into my retirement from the Federal Air Marshal Service. Although my life's pace has changed considerably, I will always remain an ardent student of violence and the predatory mindset. Over the last twenty-eight years, the study of violence has become a big part of who I am. The realities of human behavior formed the filter through which I viewed the rest of the world. Now, in retirement, I have the advantage of viewing my experiences from a different perspective, that of introspection. In doing so, I see that I owe much of my success in the field of counterterrorism and law enforcement to authors whose writings provided me a firm foundation for the study of our adversaries. I will forever be indebted to Lt. Col. Dave Grossman, Loren Christensen, Gavin De Becker, and Rory Miller. Their writings provided the education I needed to be successful at my job and to provide an environment where my family could live safely, free from fear, and for that I thank you.

I also owe a huge debt of gratitude to the talented professionals at YMAA Publications. My first book, *Spotting Danger Before It Spots You*, was a best book awards finalist in 2020, and my second book, *Spotting Danger Before It Spots Your Kids*, is ready to hit the shelves.

None of this would have been possible without such a fantastic team standing behind my work.

As always, thank you to David Ripianzi, Doran Hunter, and Tim Comrie. Your input and guidance have made this series something that I would never have imagined on my own.

Thank you to my publicists Barbara Langley and Gene Ching for helping get the word out on what I feel is such an important topic. From you, I've learned that there's much more to writing a book than putting words on paper. There's a whole big world out there waiting to be reached, and finding my audience would have been impossible without you.

This third book in the series is geared specifically toward parents who want their adolescent children to be more aware of their surroundings and conscious of their own safety. As a parent of three (all now adults), I write this book with the benefit of hindsight. I completely understand the hurdles you face as parents and sympathize with some of the struggles you're bound to encounter. I owe one hundred percent of that understanding to my three beautiful children, Joshua, Elda, and Emily. Now that you're all adults, I think it's safe to say that I've learned as much from you as you'll ever learn from me. Thank you, and I love you.

Finally, thank you to my lovely wife, Kelly. You did all the heavy lifting when it came to caring for our kids. While I was bouncing around the globe, you managed to raise three loving, productive, responsible children. I appreciate everything you do. You are amazing!

Bibliography

Books and Journals

Blaskovits, B., and C. Bennell. "Are We Revealing Hidden Aspects of Our Personality When We Walk?" *Journal of Nonverbal Behavior* 43 (2019): 329–356.

De Becker, Gavin. *The Gift of Fear: Survival Signals That Protect Us from Violence.* New York: Dell Publishing, 1997.

De Becker, Gavin. *Protecting the Gift, Keeping Children and Teenagers Safe (and Parents Sane).* New York: Dell Publishing, 1999.

Web Articles and Videos

Benjamin, Ann E. "The Importance of Family Teamwork." *Metro Family.* https://www.metrofamilymagazine.com/the-importance-of-family-teamwork/.

Children's Wellness Center. "Leaving Your Child Home Alone: A Safety Preparation Guide." https://www.childrenswellnesscenter.com/2020/01/22/leaving-your-child-home-alone-a-safety-preparation-guide/.

Ehmke, Rachel. "Tips for Communicating with Your Teen." Childmind.org. https://childmind.org/article/tips-communicating-with-teen/.

EurekAlert!. "The Spotlight on Attention Is More Like a Strobe." August 22nd, 2018. https://www.eurekalert.org/pub_releases/2018-08/pu-tso081718.php.

Fairburn, Richard. "Coopers Colors: A Simple System for Situational Awareness." PoliceOne.com. Updated July 21, 2017. https://www.policeone.com/police-trainers/articles/2188253-Coopers-colors-A-simple-system-for-situational-awareness/.

Gongala, Sarari. "Teen Rebellion: Why Do They Rebel and How to Deal with It." *Mom Junction*. June 8th, 2021. https://www.momjunction.com/articles/teen-rebellion_00389300/.

Hightower, Tracy A. "Boyd's OODA Loop and How We Use It."

National Highway Traffic Safety Administration. "Pedestrian Safety." https://www.nhtsa.gov/road-safety/pedestrian-safety

Oscar Schwartz, "No, The Internet Has Not Destroyed Our Attention Spans." Theoutline.com. August 22nd, 2018. https://theoutline.com/post/5969/we-never-had-attention-spans-to-begin-with.

Pew Research Center. "Raising Kids and Running a Household: How Working Parents Share the Load." November 4th, 2015. https://www.pewresearch.org/social-trends/2015/11/04/raising-kids-and-running-a-household-how-working-parents-share-the-load/.

Stanford Children's Health. "Keeping Your Cool When Parenting Teens." https://www.stanfordchildrens.org/en/topic/default?id=keeping-your-cool-when-parenting-teens-1-2839.

Tactical Response. https://www.tacticalresponse.com/blogs/library/18649427-boyd-s-o-o-d-a-loop-and-how-we-use-it

United States Census Bureau. "Income and Poverty in the United States: 2019." https://www.census.gov/library/publications/2020/demo/p60-270.html.

Watson, Josh. "Why Is Teen Identity Development Important?" Aspiro.com. December 11th, 2019. https://aspiroadventure.com/blog/why-is-teen-identity-development-important/.

WHYY. "Brain Study Offers Insight into Teen Groupthink," February 3rd, 2011. https://whyy.org/articles/risk/.

World Health Organization. "Youth Violence." June 8th, 2020. https://www.who.int/news-room/fact-sheets/detail/youth-violence.

Youth.gov. "Sexual Exploitation & Sex Trafficking of Minors." https://youth.gov/youth-topics/trafficking-of-youth/sexual-exploitation-and-sex-trafficking.

Index

About the Author

GARY QUESENBERRY was born in the Blue Ridge Mountains of Virginia. His love of the outdoors and patriotic spirit led him to enlist in the United States Army where he served as an artilleryman during Operation Desert Storm. Gary later became a career Federal Air Marshal where he devoted his life to studying violence and predatory behavior. Now Gary has retired from federal service and serves as the CEO of  Quesenberry Personal Defense Training LLC. There he's developed numerous basic and advanced level training courses focused on mental toughness, and defensive tactics. He has an extensive background in domestic and foreign counterterror training and has worked in both the private and corporate sectors to help educate others on the importance of situational awareness and personal safety. He once again resides in his hometown in Carroll County, Virginia.

Photo by Mary McIlvaine

www.garyquesenberry.com

BOOKS FROM YMAA

101 REFLECTIONS ON TAI CHI CHUAN
108 INSIGHTS INTO TAI CHI CHUAN
A WOMAN'S QIGONG GUIDE
ADVANCING IN TAE KWON DO
ANALYSIS OF SHAOLIN CHIN NA 2ND ED
ANCIENT CHINESE WEAPONS
ART AND SCIENCE OF STAFF FIGHTING
THE ART AND SCIENCE OF SELF-DEFENSE
ART AND SCIENCE OF STICK FIGHTING
ART OF HOJO UNDO
ARTHRITIS RELIEF, 3D ED.
BACK PAIN RELIEF, 2ND ED.
BAGUAZHANG, 2ND ED.
BRAIN FITNESS
CHIN NA IN GROUND FIGHTING
CHINESE FAST WRESTLING
CHINESE FITNESS
CHINESE TUI NA MASSAGE
COMPLETE MARTIAL ARTIST
COMPREHENSIVE APPLICATIONS OF SHAOLIN CHIN NA
CONFLICT COMMUNICATION
DAO DE JING: A QIGONG INTERPRETATION
DAO IN ACTION
DEFENSIVE TACTICS
DIRTY GROUND
DR. WU'S HEAD MASSAGE
ESSENCE OF SHAOLIN WHITE CRANE
EXPLORING TAI CHI
FACING VIOLENCE
FIGHT LIKE A PHYSICIST
THE FIGHTER'S BODY
FIGHTER'S FACT BOOK 1&2
FIGHTING ARTS
FIGHTING THE PAIN RESISTANT ATTACKER
FIRST DEFENSE
FORCE DECISIONS: A CITIZENS GUIDE
INSIDE TAI CHI
JUDO ADVANTAGE
JUJI GATAME ENCYCLOPEDIA
KARATE SCIENCE
KATA AND THE TRANSMISSION OF KNOWLEDGE
KRAV MAGA COMBATIVES
KRAV MAGA FUNDAMENTAL STRATEGIES
KRAV MAGA PROFESSIONAL TACTICS
KRAV MAGA WEAPON DEFENSES
LITTLE BLACK BOOK OF VIOLENCE
LIUHEBAFA FIVE CHARACTER SECRETS
MARTIAL ARTS OF VIETNAM
MARTIAL ARTS INSTRUCTION
MARTIAL WAY AND ITS VIRTUES
MEDITATIONS ON VIOLENCE
MERIDIAN QIGONG EXERCISES
MINDFUL EXERCISE
MIND INSIDE TAI CHI
MIND INSIDE YANG STYLE TAI CHI CHUAN
NATURAL HEALING WITH QIGONG
NORTHERN SHAOLIN SWORD, 2ND ED.
OKINAWA'S COMPLETE KARATE SYSTEM: ISSHIN RYU
PRINCIPLES OF TRADITIONAL CHINESE MEDICINE
PROTECTOR ETHIC
QIGONG FOR HEALTH & MARTIAL ARTS 2ND ED.
QIGONG FOR TREATING COMMON AILMENTS

QIGONG MASSAGE
QIGONG MEDITATION: EMBRYONIC BREATHING
QIGONG GRAND CIRCULATION
QIGONG MEDITATION: SMALL CIRCULATION
QIGONG, THE SECRET OF YOUTH: DA MO'S CLASSICS
REDEMPTION
ROOT OF CHINESE QIGONG, 2ND ED.
SAMBO ENCYCLOPEDIA
SCALING FORCE
SELF-DEFENSE FOR WOMEN
SHIN GI TAI: KARATE TRAINING
SIMPLE CHINESE MEDICINE
SIMPLE QIGONG EXERCISES FOR HEALTH, 3RD ED.
SIMPLIFIED TAI CHI CHUAN, 2ND ED.
SOLO TRAINING 1&2
SPOTTING DANGER BEFORE IT SPOTS YOU
SPOTTING DANGER BEFORE IT SPOTS YOUR KIDS
SPOTTING DANGER BEFORE IT SPOTS YOUR TEENS
SUMO FOR MIXED MARTIAL ARTS
SUNRISE TAI CHI
SURVIVING ARMED ASSAULTS
TAE KWON DO: THE KOREAN MARTIAL ART
TAEKWONDO BLACK BELT POOMSAE
TAEKWONDO: A PATH TO EXCELLENCE
TAEKWONDO: ANCIENT WISDOM
TAEKWONDO: DEFENSE AGAINST WEAPONS
TAEKWONDO: SPIRIT AND PRACTICE
TAI CHI BALL QIGONG: FOR HEALTH AND MARTIAL ARTS
TAI CHI BALL WORKOUT FOR BEGINNERS
THE TAI CHI BOOK
TAI CHI CHIN NA, 2ND ED.
TAI CHI CHUAN CLASSICAL YANG STYLE, 2ND ED.
TAI CHI CHUAN MARTIAL POWER, 3RD ED.
TAI CHI CONCEPTS AND EXPERIMENTS
TAI CHI CONNECTIONS
TAI CHI DYNAMICS
TAI CHI FOR DEPRESSION
TAI CHI IN 10 WEEKS
TAI CHI PUSH HANDS
TAI CHI QIGONG, 3RD ED.
TAI CHI SECRETS OF THE ANCIENT MASTERS
TAI CHI SECRETS OF THE WU & LI STYLES
TAI CHI SECRETS OF THE WU STYLE
TAI CHI SECRETS OF THE YANG STYLE
TAI CHI SWORD: CLASSICAL YANG STYLE, 2ND ED.
TAI CHI SWORD FOR BEGINNERS
TAI CHI WALKING
TAIJIQUAN THEORY OF DR. YANG, JWING-MING
FIGHTING ARTS
TRADITIONAL CHINESE HEALTH SECRETS
TRADITIONAL TAEKWONDO
TRAINING FOR SUDDEN VIOLENCE
TRIANGLE HOLD ENCYCLOPEDIA
TRUE WELLNESS SERIES (MIND, HEART, GUT)
WARRIOR'S MANIFESTO
WAY OF KATA
WAY OF SANCHIN KATA
WAY TO BLACK BELT
WESTERN HERBS FOR MARTIAL ARTISTS
WILD GOOSE QIGONG
WINNING FIGHTS
XINGYIQUAN

AND MANY MORE . . .

VIDEOS FROM YMAA

AND MANY MORE . . .

more products available from . . .
YMAA Publication Center, Inc. 楊氏東方文化出版中心
1-800-669-8892 • info@ymaa.com • www.ymaa.com